Reflections of the
University of Leicester

 **University** *of*
Leicester

**Presented to graduates of University College, Leicester
to celebrate 90 years of academic excellence in Leicester
1921-2011**

Professor Sir Robert Burgess

Joanne Wood

Reflections of
the University of Leicester

Robert G. Burgess and Joanne Wood

UNIVERSITY OF LEICESTER PRESS

First published in 2010 by University of Leicester Press
University Road
Leicester
LE1 7RH

ISBN 978-0-9564739-0-5

British Library Cataloguing in Publication Data

A catalogue record for this book is available from the British Library

Cover Illustrations
Front: Reflections of the Engineering Building in the glass front of the David Wilson
Library, University of Leicester.
Back: Senior staff and honorary graduates celebrate the end of the degree ceremonies in
July 2006.

For our parents

Contents

Preface

This book is a commemorative volume published to celebrate the 50th Anniversary of the University of Leicester gaining university status. The choice of images is designed to provide an insight into the diverse range of activities which constitute the University over the fifty year period from 1957/58 to 2007/08. Unlike other publications on higher education institutions, our book departs from the standard historical account as we wanted to produce a volume with a difference that illustrated diverse aspects of university life.

When we set out to write this book, we thought it would be easy; how wrong we were! Providing an insight into the diverse range of activities that constitute the University of Leicester has undoubtedly been a challenge. While we had expected the task of identifying the major themes over a fifty year period to be somewhat demanding, we did not expect the sourcing and selection of material to be as difficult as it has proved – perhaps our expectations of the quantity and quality of images were somewhat high at the start of this project.

Universities have much to celebrate and the University of Leicester is no exception. The images we have chosen depict the wide range of activities in which members of the University have been involved, some of which you may have expected to see and others which are less conventional. In addition, we convey how the different people involved with the University are its greatest asset. We believe that it is important to demonstrate that the University is a well-rounded organisation which has its share of 'ups and downs', all adding to the rich pattern of life. Altogether it is this variety which has shaped the development and character of the University. It will, we hope, remind members of the community of the excitements and frustrations involved in taking the institution forward.

We have picked out some of the key themes at the heart of the University including celebration, community, teaching and research to demonstrate what has been achieved over the past fifty years. We also give a brief account of its earlier origins as a University College as well as giving a flavour of some potential future developments. However, this material is deliberately not presented in a strict chronological order as it was not our intention that this should be a history of the University. While a book such as this may be read from cover to cover it can also be dipped into as the Chapters provide accounts and pictures of different aspects of the University community. Overall, we hope that, whatever way our book is used, you will enjoy learning a little more about the life and work of the University of Leicester over the past fifty years and gain an insight into what life within one of Britain's leading higher education institutions is really like.

Robert G. Burgess and Joanne Wood
University of Leicester

Acknowledgements

The authors would like to thank the following people, without whose assistance the book would not have been produced. We were very fortunate to have a number of people who were willing to read and comment in some detail on an earlier version: Hilary Burgess; Peter Durham; Gordon Fyfe; Ken Pounds; and Linda Rudkin. We have benefited from their comments and taken many on board to improve this publication. Obviously, any errors or omissions are our own.

Within the University, numerous people have helped in answering our questions and queries during the course of this project. We would particularly like to thank Angela Chorley for her hard work, creativity and imagination in designing and typesetting the book. Mary Bettles and Alex Cave were invaluable in our endeavours to find material from the University of Leicester archive. Our thanks should also go to Colin Brooks who has taken, and provided copies of, many of the photographs and Ron Kimms who supplied numerous photographs on the early years of the University which he has very carefully assembled and gifted to the University.

Finally, we would also like to thank the secretarial staff within the Vice-Chancellor's Office who cheered us on and frequently provided us with much needed refreshment while completing this publication, as well as numerous colleagues in academic departments and in Corporate Services.

Note on Illustrations

Unless otherwise stated, all the illustrations are from the University of Leicester's Archive, and the University of Leicester is the copyright holder. The University has acted in good faith and made reasonable efforts to gain permission from other copyright holders, for which we are very grateful, including: Adrian Beck, Andrew Willis and Palgrave Macmillan; Nick Carter, Keith Perch and the *Leicester Mercury*; Martine Hamilton Knight; the Lord Chamberlain's Office; John McKean and Phaidon Press; The Press Association; Stephen Rench, Oxfordshire Studies [© Images & Voices, Oxfordshire County Council – Thomas Photos]; The Royal Mail; Professor Sarah Spurgeon; and Patrick White and Palgrave Macmillan. If any pictures have been wrongly attributed we ask the legitimate rights holder to contact the University.

Introduction

In the fifty years since the University of Leicester was established 100,000 students from around the globe have graduated. It has moved a long way from being a small provincial college that offered a limited range of degree programmes validated by the University of London up until the late 1950s. Students in the graduating class of 1958 were given the option of choosing to accept a degree either from the University of London or from the newly established University of Leicester following the award of the Royal Charter.

The development of a University in Leicester fulfilled the ambitions of many local citizens in the late-19th and early-20th centuries who had made the case for higher education to be provided in the city. During a time of post-World War I optimism, and in common with many other industrial cities at the time, local professional people wanted to establish a University, believing that it would bring prosperity, employment and increased educational opportunities to the area. They argued that the presence of a University would result in a well educated population which would contribute to the professions in the immediate area and thereby contribute to economic development locally and regionally. Their optimism was well founded as many University initiatives have contributed directly to Leicester, Leicestershire and Rutland. For example, the School of Education has supplied teachers to numerous local schools and the Medical School has trained many doctors who have subsequently become hospital consultants or general practitioners locally. Similarly, Leicester has launched the careers of many lawyers, social workers, accountants and other professionals who have taken up roles in the city and neighbouring counties.

Higher education provision in Leicester was always broadly based in the arts and sciences and remains so in the 21st century. Thus, many disciplines are represented in Leicester's undergraduate and postgraduate curricula which are firmly underpinned by major research activity. Indeed, the University has become a leading international research-intensive institution offering numerous programmes in subjects as diverse as Biochemistry, Computer Science, Economics, Law and History of Art.

All Leicester's departments have developed high quality work over the last fifty years. They have achieved this by contributing to the development of their disciplines, vocational and professional activities through research and teaching at undergraduate and postgraduate levels on campus and through distance learning. In this book, we set out to highlight some of these activities by addressing a series of questions in the Chapters that follow:

Chapter One (Foundations)

How did a University come to be developed in Leicester? What were its origins? Who was involved in its establishment? What was the shape of the academic curriculum? What academic structures were developed? How did University College Leicester influence the development of the University?

Chapter Two (Developments)

In what ways has the University developed its estate? Who were the benefactors? What was the pattern of building development? Who were the major architects? How have academic initiatives influenced the shape and style of buildings?

Chapter Three (Teaching and Learning)

How has the curriculum been defined? What approaches were taken to teaching? What styles of formal and informal learning have been used? Has teaching and learning increased in status? What major pedagogic developments have taken place?

Chapter Four (Research)

What are the major research strengths of the University? How have they advanced? Who has initiated them? What links does the University have with industry? How has Leicester's research contributed to scientific and medical developments? What has been the role of inter-disciplinary work and how might it be taken forward?

Chapter Five (People)

Who have been the people associated with the progress of the University? Who are the unsung heroes that keep the University running? Who are the people who have been essential to the University's success? Which academic staff have made major contributions within and beyond Leicester? How have students contributed to the life of the academic community?

Chapter Six (Communities)

How is the University involved in Leicester, Leicestershire and Rutland? How has the University contributed to the development of the area? What contribution has the University made to major local initiatives such as the National Space Centre? What voluntary activities does the University engage in and how do they contribute to the wellbeing of the local community?

Chapter Seven (Celebrations)

What has the University celebrated in its fifty year history? What celebrations occur annually? Do staff and student celebrations differ in style? What special events have involved major celebrations? What staff have had major achievements to celebrate? What does the University have to celebrate by way of success?

In addressing these issues we have selected a wide range of photographs that illustrate major recurring themes in the life of the University and demonstrate the diverse range of activity that makes up Leicester. These photographs also illustrate changes – from the relatively superficial, like styles of dress – to other major changes such as teaching methods, technological developments and their applications. They also illustrate major societal shifts such as the greater representation of women staff and students together with an increased number of international students studying on and off-campus over the fifty year period. The student body is now more diverse, the teaching and learning opportunities have increased and the volume of research activity has grown dramatically. Leicester is therefore not only well known locally but also nationally and internationally. However, some aspects of the culture endure and certain features of the compact campus and the curriculum remain highly recognisable. It is widely known for its work in Genetics, Museum Studies, Archaeology and Ancient History, Economics and Physics and Astronomy. It has also been portrayed anonymously in a number of campus novels including Kingsley Amis's *Lucky Jim* and Malcolm Bradbury's *Eating People is Wrong* which, like many other novels in this genre, provide an intriguing insight into University life.

In common with many universities, members of staff and former students have also produced historical accounts of the University and its development. Jack Simmons, the founding Professor of History, wrote *New University* in 1958 which provided an account of the early development of University College while Brenda Bullock provided a student perspective of the University in *Over the Wall: A Working Class Girl at University in the 1950s*. Subsequently Brian Burch produced a volume entitled *The University of Leicester – A History 1921-1996* in which he traced the origins of the institution, its transition from a College to a University and developments in the modern era. Our book departs from this historical narrative and provides a visual account of major activities in Leicester whilst highlighting how all members of the University, regardless of their occupation or subject of study, have contributed significantly to its success. Certainly, the University has justified the arguments advanced by the 'founding fathers' who developed the case for a University of Leicester. We are all immensely proud of the long-standing, rich legacy that the University has contributed and which is reflected in this book.

1. Foundations

The case for establishing higher education in the City of Leicester was at the heart of public debate in the latter part of the nineteenth century. Many local groups including the Literary and Philosophical Society, with whom the University still has a close relationship, were instrumental in contributing to a wide range of debates through meetings and lectures which discussed the case for higher education in Leicester. This was recognised and supported by a range of distinguished local people including politicians and professionals such as Sir Jonathan North, Dr Astley Clarke, Sir Samuel Faire and Percy Gee.

These individuals and many others worked tirelessly to develop higher education provision in the City. Indeed, a number of University buildings bear their names and as a consequence many of them are still well known on the Leicester campus.

There are many other aspects of the University of Leicester today that have links with the past and have shaped its style: architecturally, organisationally and in the curriculum, the teaching programme and in some research activities. University College Leicester, which opened in 1921 with nine students, had many features which were understandably taken up by the University of Leicester when it was established in the late 1950s. Students of University College were, in common with students in many university colleges throughout the country, prepared for external degrees of the University of London as well as being trained to be teachers. Today many of these former students see themselves as Leicester alumni as they identify with the University Road site and some of its original buildings, even though these have been modified over the years and now form part of the University of Leicester.

At the time Leicester established University College other cities had also developed colleges of this kind offering external degrees from the University of London. These included Reading, Southampton and Nottingham, all of which had strong local support and eventually made the case to develop their colleges into independent universities that were civic in style, as a result of their strong local connections. Some, such as Nottingham, were fortunate enough to have wealthy benefactors who were able to invest heavily in land and buildings. In Leicester's case, the principal benefactor was local businessman Thomas Fielding Johnson who provided thirty seven acres of land for educational purposes of which six were provided to establish University College. The remaining thirty one acres were given to set up grammar schools for boys and girls. In addition, there were individual benefactions from local manufacturers in the hosiery industry and in local footwear companies, albeit not on the same scale as Jesse Boot was able to offer to Nottingham. The College therefore had a presence in the City on a very compact site – a feature still associated with the contemporary University of Leicester.

The focal point of University College was the 'Main Building' (now the Fielding Johnson Building) which had been the Leicestershire and Rutland Lunatic Asylum in the 19th century. Its architectural drawings provide clues to the composition of the staff and the academic curriculum. From the outset, arts and science subjects were taught. Botany and Zoology were offered from the early years, as were Chemistry and Physics. These have always remained among Leicester's great strengths in science. Education was a separate department and Vaughan College, the former Working Men's College, was a separate institution associated with the teaching of adult students. It merged with University College in the early 1930s. This subsequently became an important feature of the University of Leicester through the provision of adult education classes organised in Leicester and Northampton by the Department of Adult Education and latterly the Institute of Lifelong Learning. The College's curriculum continued to develop across the humanities and the sciences and it was keen to start offering a number of new courses including Medicine. However, this development did not come to fruition until the University's Medical School was established in the 1970s, making a positive difference to local health provision.

The first Principal, Dr Robert Rattray, was instrumental in introducing a wide-ranging curriculum which was expanded by Frederick Attenborough, Leicester's second Principal. Attenborough also began the appointment of Professorial staff, first in Education, Adult Education and Chemistry and then a further group of Professorial appointments in Physics, History and English. However, it was Charles Wilson, the College's last Principal and first Vice-Chancellor of the University, who was to further develop the Professoriate. He was principally responsible for increasing the scale of the site by adding further buildings, some of which were constructed after he had completed his period of office in Leicester.

There were many developments in University College that have continued to mould the shape, style and character of the University of Leicester. They include:

- building developments on University Road (the academic campus) and Oadby (the residential estate);
- the acquisition of Knighton Hall by Frederick Attenborough who considered this to be an ideal residence to replace College House for future Vice-Chancellors;
- the establishment of the role of Chancellor (replacing that of President in University College);
- the development of a University structure based on Faculties headed by Deans that was established in 1951 and reviewed in 2008 when it was agreed it should be replaced by a College structure with Pro-Vice-Chancellors as Heads of Colleges;
- the use of the site as a location for major conferences including the British Association for the Advancement of Science;
- a Students' Union that has had close affiliation with the National Union of Students since the mid-1920s;
- the development of a RAG week that marked charitable work by the Students' Union for the local community which continues to this day and is augmented by a range of other voluntary activities by students; and
- the breadth of the curriculum across the arts, science, medicine, biological sciences, law and the social sciences.

These, and many other, characteristics remain in the modern University and, unlike the green-field site campus universities of the 1960s, the universities that emerged from university colleges strongly reflect their origins in terms of governance, organisation, breadth of academic provision, teaching and research. These features constitute the legacy of Leicester which will be explored in subsequent chapters.

The Early Days: University College Leicester

1-2. There were many benefactors and key players in the early development of University College, not least Thomas Fielding Johnson who gave the Leicestershire and Rutland Lunatic Asylum to the City.

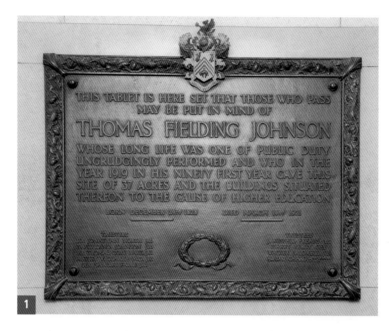

3. The Fielding Johnson Building once had a more interesting use as the Leicestershire and Rutland Lunatic Asylum. Subsequently, it became the home of the Leicester, Leicestershire and Rutland College and much of the teaching took place in this building which has subsequently had many uses. Currently, it is the home of Corporate Services although some say that, in keeping with its origins, it still houses a somewhat eclectic mix of people! This picture shows the Leicestershire and Rutland Lunatic Asylum, from a drawing by T Willson, engraved by H Adlard, 1849.

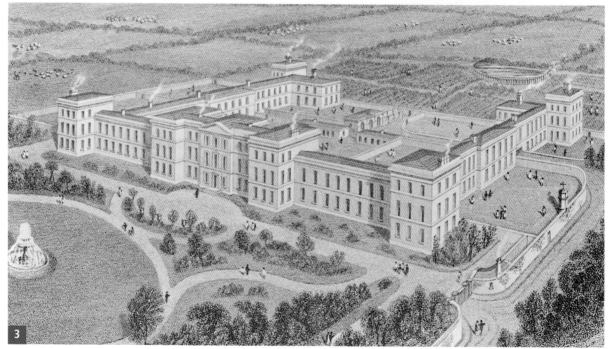

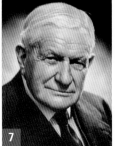

4. The first Principal of University College, Dr Robert Rattray (seated centre), pictured with a group of students and some staff members in the summer of 1922.

5-8. Sir Jonathan North (5), Dr Astley Clarke (6), H Percy Gee (7) and Dr FW Bennett (8) were all key people who actively participated in the establishment of the College and its subsequent development as many of them were supporters, benefactors and chairs of College Council.

9. A cartoon from the Leicester Mail in May 1923 portrays some of the key people involved in the unveiling of a mural tablet and opening of the College Library.

10-11. One of the rooms that is well known to generations of University staff and students is the Gimson Room. It is named after Ernest Gimson, a local craftsman whose student produced the furniture shown in the picture. He was well-known nationally as part of the Arts and Crafts Movement. The furniture remains in situ today, although the décor looks very different, and the room is currently used as a major boardroom.

12. Royal visits to the site in University Road began early in the life of University College. HRH The Prince of Wales visited University College in March 1927. Here he is seen with Dr Rattray prior to planting a tree in the College grounds.

13-15. The first RAG event was held on Shrove Tuesday in 1930 when College students organised a Pancake Riot, which was described as a 'public demonstration of hooliganism' by one irate letter-writer in the local press. These events have continued down the years, greatly enjoyed by many students but not necessarily by the citizens of Leicester! In 1949 one student, Alan Warren, commented 'That grass skirt lasted me (and our garden) until I retired in 1988!' and in 1951 the students became renowned for stealing the London School of Economics' mascot, the Beaver. (15)

16. From the very beginning of University College, conferences and events have been part of the calendar. In 1933 the British Association of Science held its annual meeting at the College and a garden party on the lawn outside the Fielding Johnson Building.

17. In 1956 Percy Gee, shown with three Dutch nuns, hosted a reception for overseas students taking a vacation course in English Language, Literature and Education for Overseas Students.

LEICESTER EVENING MAIL, DECEMBER 5, 1946.

Leicester Evening Mail

11227: THURSDAY, DECEMBER 5, 1946.   THREE-HALFPENCE

Strikers' Plea To Leicester M.P.s

FINAL

BEGOWNED STUDENTS IN COLLEGE PICKET

LEICESTER University College students who came out on strike last night in protest against the "outside" appointments of professors, today sent letters to the Minister of Education and the three Leicester MPs asking for support.

The Principal of the College, Mr. F. L. Attenborough, who is taking no action in the strike, told the Evening Mail that the appointment of a professor was made in accordance with the conditions laid down by the University Grants Committee.

Today, in the icy cold, students wrapped in scarves, some wearing their gowns, picketed the gates of the College.

Only one student attempted to elude them, and today he was the solitary occupant of the chemistry laboratory, where he is taking an examination.

Mr. Attenborough told the Evening Mail that some time ago the College decided to apply to the University Grants Committee for assistance in establishing a number of chairs.

The Grants Committee was a national body, with Sir Walter Moberley as chairman, and comprising a number of distinguished men and women.

They received money from the Treasury for the purpose of extending University education and passed it on to universities after much consideration.

(continued on Page 2)

STUDENTS picketing one of the gates of Leicester University College

18-19. For many years the word 'student' was often associated with strikes and demonstrations. Even before Leicester became a University, students were involved in these activities, for example, in December 1946 all students bar one came out on strike to protest against the decision to appoint professors from outside the University instead of staff who were already at University College. In addition, they sent letters of protest to the Minister of Education and Leicester MPs.

EXTRA
Leicester Mercury
★ LARGEST CERTIFIED NET SALE ★
Established 1874   THURSDAY, DECEMBER 5th, 1946   Three-Half-Pence

Dr. A. S. Collins   Mr. Attenborough.

'ABSURD TO THINK THEY SHOULD PRESUME TO CHOOSE STAFF'——COLLEGE PRINCIPAL

STUDENTS ON STRIKE—ALL BUT ONE

Mr. C. Nutting (left) a chemistry student, passing the pickets in the University College grounds. He was the only student at work to-day

'Poor Show,' Said The Pickets, And Let Him Pass

In the otherwise empty laboratory of Leicester University College, one student was taking his terminal examination to-day. All the other classrooms were deserted. Outside, students College gowns, some of them girls, were picketing the grounds in the first day of the students' protest strike against two outside appointments to professional (?professorial) chairs.

Miss Sheila Harris addressing students at UCL to-day

20-21. In the 1950s, the Students' Union held an annual dinner in one of the halls of residence which, in common with most activities at this time, was a formal event (at least from the perspective of the 21st century).

22. Today, annual celebrations take the form of a Summer Ball, a very different type of occasion with fireworks, live bands and side shows. Student events today lack the formality of the 1950s and continue well into the night. The 1am finish in the 1950s is more likely to be 4am in the twenty-first century.

23. The Library has always been at the heart of the College and the University. In 1952 the College Library contained more than 75,000 volumes and was accommodated in the Fielding Johnson Building. Subsequently it was extended to allow further development. In 2008, the David Wilson Library houses one million volumes and is a state-of-the-art facility with electronic and paper publications available for the benefit of staff and students, some of which have been donated.

24. Research and development work took place in the laboratories in University College. In the early 1950s, the Physics Department was involved in experimental research and built this million-volt Van Der Graaff generator in its workshop which was located on the ground floor of the Fielding Johnson Building and used by Dr Matsuoka for nuclear physics research.

25. Many buildings in University Road are instantly recognised by alumni. While the exteriors may be familiar, the teaching and research that takes place within them will usually have changed. The Astley Clarke Building, which now houses Economics, was originally the Biological Sciences Building housing laboratories, research rooms and a large lecture theatre for the Departments of Botany and Zoology. The Department of Biology is now located in the Adrian Building which has undergone considerable refurbishment to bring its facilities into the twenty-first century.

26. The second Principal of University College was Frederick Attenborough, the father of Lord Richard (pictured), Sir David and John. The whole family have very fond memories of their time at Leicester and have continued to provide great support to the University.

27-28. Student life has been organised over the years by the Student Representative Council and, in turn, the Students' Union. The Student Council in 1956-57 witnessed the transition from College to University in a very different, more formal, era compared to the experiences of their counterparts in the Students' Union Sabbatical team in 2008-09. From left to right: Rob Hicks, Johanna Rigden, Dee Patel, Kirsten Dyer and Graham Ross.

The University of Leicester

ELIZABETH THE SECOND by the Grace of God of the United Kingdom of Great Britain and Northern Ireland and of Our other Realms and Territories Queen, Head of the Commonwealth, Defender of the Faith.

TO ALL TO WHOM THESE PRESENTS SHALL COME, GREETING!

WHEREAS an humble Petition has been presented to Us by the University College of Leicester praying that We should constitute and found a University within Our City and County of Leicester for the Advancement of Knowledge, the Diffusion and Extension of Arts, Sciences and Learning, the Provision of Liberal, Professional and Technological Education and for the furtherance of the objects for which the University College of Leicester was incorporated by a Charter granted by Our Royal Predecessor His Majesty King George the Sixth and dated the fourth day of December in the year of our Lord One thousand nine hundred and fifty and to grant a Charter with such provisions in that behalf as shall seem to Us right and suitable:

AND WHEREAS We have taken the said Petition into Our Royal Consideration and are minded to accede thereto:

NOW THEREFORE KNOW YE that We by virtue of Our Royal Prerogative and of Our especial grace, certain knowledge and mere motion have willed and ordained and by these Presents do for Us, Our Heirs and Successors will and ordain as follows:—

1. There shall be and there is hereby constituted and founded in Our said City and County of Leicester a University by the name and style of "The University of Leicester" with Faculties of Arts, Science, Education and the Social Sciences and such other Faculties either in addition to or in substitution for the aforesaid

Faculties or any of them as may from time to time be constituted by Statutes or Ordinances of the University.

2. Our right trusty and well beloved Edgar Douglas, Baron Adrian, Member of the Order of Merit and President of the University College of Leicester, the persons named in the First Schedule hereto as members of the Court, the Council, and the Senate, and the members for the time being of the Court, the Council, the Senate, and the Faculties of the University, the Graduates and the Undergraduates of the University, the Chancellor, the Pro-Chancellors, the Vice-Chancellor, the Treasurer, the Pro-Vice-Chancellor and the Deans of Faculties of the University for the time being and all others who shall pursuant to this Our Charter and the Statutes of the University for the time being be Members of the University are hereby constituted and from henceforth for ever shall be one body politic and corporate with perpetual succession and a Common Seal by the name and style of "The University of Leicester" (hereinafter called "the University") with full power and capacity by and in such name to sue and be sued and to take and hold land, and with power, subject to the Customs and Laws of Arms, to acquire armorial bearings which shall be duly recorded in Our College of Arms, and to do all other lawful acts whatsoever and with full right, authority, power and capacity without any further or other licence by virtue of this Our Charter to take purchase and hold such lands, tenements and hereditaments as may be for the time being occupied by or on behalf of the University for the transaction of its business and the actual carrying out of its purposes and also in addition without licence in mortmain other lands, tenements and hereditaments to the annual value

29. In 1957 University College became the University of Leicester and was granted its own degree-awarding powers by Royal Charter.

The Installation of the First Chancellor 1958

30

31

30-31. The first Chancellor of the new University, The Right Honorable the Lord Adrian OM, MA, MD, DSc, LLD, FRS, FRCP (1957-71), was installed on Friday 20 June 1958 at a ceremony in the De Montfort Hall (still used for degree ceremonies). This was a notable occasion in the University's history and Lord Adrian saw many changes during his years as Chancellor. The installation of a new Chancellor (the key honorary role) is an important event in any University's history and in the 1950s included guests from virtually every university in the UK as well as civic dignitaries.

32. *The University Gazette* reported that during Lord Adrian's installation 800 people attended a buffet lunch in the De Montfort Hall gardens followed by a Garden Party at Beaumont Hall attended by 700 people. In the evening 430 people attended a dinner to round off this momentous occasion. The University has since been fortunate to have distinguished figures taking on the role:

   1971-84 Professor Sir Alan Hodgkin, OM, KBE, MA, ScD, MD, DSc, FRS
   1984-95 The Lord Porter, OM, FRS, BSc, MA PhD, ScD, FRSC
   1995-05 Sir Michael Atiyah, OM, FRS, MA, PhD, DSc
   2005-   Sir Peter Williams, CBE, FRS, FREng

33. However, it is the Vice-Chancellor who is responsible for the day-to-day running of the University. The first Vice-Chancellor, Sir Charles Wilson MA, LLD (1957-61), was most remembered for completing more building projects and establishing more professorships than either of the previous College Principals. He took a great interest in encouraging students' independence. This development has continued under subsequent Vice-Chancellors, all of whom are portrayed in later Chapters:

   1962-76 Sir Fraser Noble, MBE, MA, LLD
   1977-87 Sir Maurice Shock, MA, LLD
   1987-99 Dr K J R Edwards, BSc, MA, PhD, DSc, LLD
   1999-   Professor Sir Robert Burgess, BA, PhD, AcSS

34. University College developed over thirty-six years and the site around University Road and Victoria Park continues to be recognisable, although the activities within its constituent buildings have evolved as the subsequent chapters will demonstrate.

2. Developments

The original land and buildings were given to University College by Thomas Fielding Johnson who made many similar donations across the City, including the Fielding Johnson Hospital on Waterloo Way (that subsequently became the Norwich Union building). Although many people make reference to the fact that the Fielding Johnson Building was a lunatic asylum before it was handed over to University College, few are aware that the current Council Chamber is the asylum's former Chapel!

The original building housed all the academic developments on the site until a case was made for the College to become a University in its own right. During the 1950s, the Principal, Charles Wilson, engaged in a building programme which helped to demonstrate that more students and activities could be accommodated on the site. It was during this time that the Astley Clarke and Percy Gee buildings were developed. Some of the original buildings were also demolished when accommodation was transferred to the Knighton site, albeit mainly residential properties such as the original College Hall. It was at this time that the Oadby estate was also acquired, although its development did not occur immediately.

When the College became a University, Charles Wilson became its first Vice-Chancellor and campus development continued to take place using his original Masterplan, developed with the distinguished architect, Sir Leslie Martin who was appointed as the consultant for the development of the site. His advice was not always taken however; in particular when the University decided to modify some of his proposals for the development of the Biological Sciences Building. There have, over the years, been many times in the University's history when parts of the campus have resembled a building site and, as a consequence, staff and students have needed to be extremely tolerant whilst changes have taken place. However, staff have always wanted to move with the times and readily extend their activities, so they have always appreciated the need for development and the resultant benefits when buildings were constructed. Notable amongst these are the Medical School with its modern laboratories, named after Sir Maurice Shock (a former Vice-Chancellor), and the Robert Kilpatrick Clinical Sciences Building on the Leicester Royal Infirmary site (named after a former Dean of Medicine). All these developments have improved not only the facilities available to staff and students but also the aesthetics of the campus. Peter Sneath (a retired professor), who has been with the University since its early days, was heard to comment at the opening of the Henry Wellcome Building that he never thought he would see such good laboratories in the University, as he had been very pleased with the Medical School's original provision.

Another key feature of many university campuses is that their buildings have become part of the nation's heritage. For example, Leicester's Engineering Building designed by James Stirling and James Gowan is widely recognised as being the first building designed in Britain after the modernist era. It is a listed building and, as a consequence, is regularly visited by architectural students, historical societies and members of the public keen to see this fine example of Stirling and Gowan's work.

It is well known that all universities have contrasting styles of architecture which, like them or loathe them, are distinctive of the period in which they were designed; much of which was in the 1970s. Leicester's architecture includes some Denys Lasdun buildings, such as the Charles Wilson Building and Stamford Hall. Lasdun was another well-known architect whose work can also be seen at the University of East Anglia (where he had worked with Charles Wilson who headed that University's Development Committee) and the University of London's Institute of Education. A further addition to Leicester's iconic buildings is the £32 million David Wilson Library which was designed by Associated Architects, chosen as the architectural practice with considerable experience in converting existing buildings, modernising them and integrating them with 'new build'. In particular, members of the University were aware of their innovative work in Birmingham where they had converted a Royal Mail Sorting Office into a distinctive shopping complex, 'The Mailbox'.

Given the high cost of new buildings, universities are also renowned for refurbishment of their existing facilities. At Leicester, for example, part of the David Wilson Library project was to renovate the existing building and double its size. The Lecture Theatre in the Attenborough teaching block was converted to a Film Theatre which can still be used for lectures. Laboratories for the Genetics Centre for Excellence in Teaching and Learning and the Geography Department's Virtual Reality Suite for its Centre for Excellence for Teaching and Learning in Spatial Literacy were all refurbishment projects. The original facilities are hardly recognisable; a testament to the high quality work undertaken by University staff and

contractors. In any large organisation there inevitably has to be a rolling programme of refurbishment and a university is no different in this respect. Teaching, research, office and residential facilities all have to be of an acceptable standard and kept up-to-date; something of a 'Forth Bridge' project for the Estates Department!

One feature of university development is that many buildings are named after people who have played a key role in the institution or are, more recently, major benefactors. Leicester, for example, has the Adrian Building (named after Lord Adrian, the first Chancellor) housing Biological Sciences; the David Wilson Library (named after its main sponsor); the Frank and Katherine May Lecture Theatre (both of whom are long-standing benefactors to the University); the George Porter Building (named after Lord Porter, the third Chancellor) housing Chemistry; the Henry Wellcome Building (named after the Trust who part-funded the project) which houses Biomedical Sciences; the Ian Lauder Clinical Skills Centre (named after a former Dean of Medicine); and the Ken Edwards Building (named after a former Vice-Chancellor) which houses the School of Management.

Another factor which drives the need for universities to expand and develop is the changing demands of their students. Certainly, students in the 21st century set very high standards and expect all manner of facilities that would not have been considered a necessity in the early days of University College. Take halls of residence, for example – students of earlier generations were highly appreciative that their accommodation had central heating, a novelty that many had not encountered at home. Today's students, however, take it for granted and also expect en-suite facilities and internet access that earlier generations could never have dreamed about. The University has managed to keep pace with changing times to satisfy the demands of students by providing high quality facilities in all areas – even the David Wilson Library toilets have their own

Appreciation Society on the social networking website Facebook! Halls are also now mixed, whereas they used to be single sex, and virtually none of the early students would have owned a car whereas today, despite environmental concerns, many students have access to a vehicle which they would like to bring with them to University even though they will be required to purchase a parking permit. Although car use is discouraged, mainly due to a lack of parking, many still bring vehicles onto campus which creates its own difficulties, not least in the competition amongst staff and students for parking spaces. Demand for car parking by staff has also increased dramatically, despite many living in the local area, as significant numbers of staff are forced to drive in from outlying areas and, for various reasons, are unable to rely on public transport.

The degree of formality in universities has also changed over the years and there is now much less distinction between staff and students. Staff no longer wear academic dress, other than for degree ceremonies, and regular informal communication occurs between staff and students through emails, blogs and so on. The style of Leicester's degree programmes has also changed as it now has almost equal numbers of postgraduate and undergraduate students including a large proportion of distance learning students. Obviously, these developments present their own challenges, such as having to provide facilities fifty two weeks of the year rather than just during the traditional thirty week academic year. This is also relevant to the Oadby campus which for many years relied heavily on conference and events business for commercial, not just academic, purposes. Regular conference business has included SAGA holidays; Terry Wogan's group of listeners and charity workers, the 'TOGs'; language schools; learned societies and academic groups.

Maintaining and developing a university campus is no mean feat and Leicester is no exception. The University has 220 properties on five major sites, with the principal sites being in the University Road and Oadby areas. One of the main campus features, however, is the density of the site and the short walking distance between buildings. The delightful setting of Victoria Park, although not owned by the University, also contributes to the overall look of the campus. In 2008 Leicester's Facebook also described the University as 'friendly' and 'a nice place', something which can only be maintained with continued development and investment in the institution's infrastructure and facilities.

The Campus

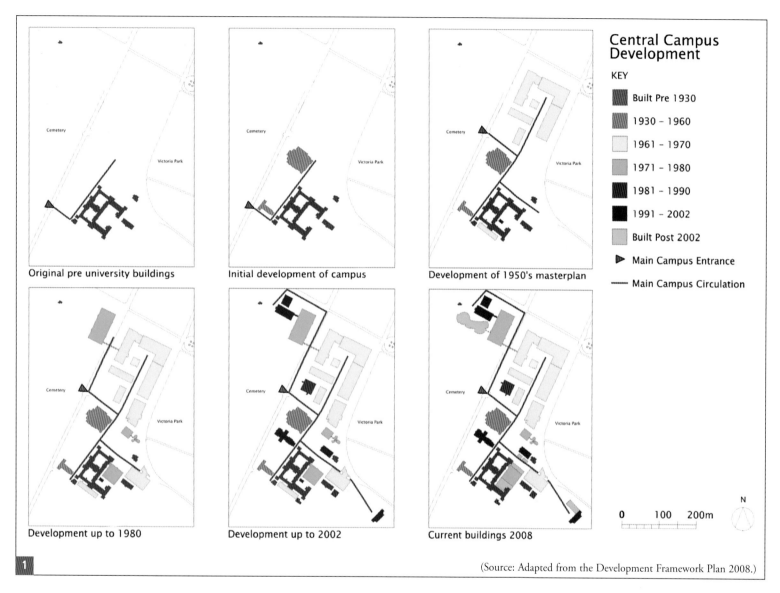

Original pre university buildings

Initial development of campus

Development of 1950's masterplan

Development up to 1980

Development up to 2002

Current buildings 2008

Central Campus Development

KEY

- Built Pre 1930
- 1930 – 1960
- 1961 – 1970
- 1971 – 1980
- 1981 – 1990
- 1991 – 2002
- Built Post 2002
- ▶ Main Campus Entrance
- —— Main Campus Circulation

0   100   200m

N

(Source: Adapted from the Development Framework Plan 2008.)

1. The steady growth of University College and the University of Leicester is well charted in a series of maps included in the University's 2008 Development Framework Plan showing the expansion of the main campus during different periods of time. In particular, the campus map reflects major national growth in higher education in the 1960s when many buildings were constructed at universities across the country, including Leicester.

Academic Buildings

2. In 1958 Leicester was in the throes of a five-year building plan which included new buildings for Chemistry and Physics. On 1 November 1958 *Ripple* reported on refurbishments which included relocating common rooms, kitchens and moving the Students' Union to the Percy Gee Building, where it remains today. In fact, this is the University's next major building project, following the completion of the Library in 2008. As with all refurbishment programmes over the years, existing buildings are transformed and become hardly recognisable to those familiar with the original site. However, as with any change, there was some criticism of the extent of the work, as in the words of the then Vice-Chancellor, it involved "musical chairs"; an unavoidable process which continues to this day.

3. On 17 May 1963 *Ripple* covered the opening of the new Adult Education centre, as an extension of the University. Located in the heart of the City, amongst the Roman remains and Jewry Wall, Vaughan College was established to provide adult education classes for a wider range of people that were drawn from different backgrounds and who wanted to develop their knowledge and understanding across a wide range of subjects taught by University staff.

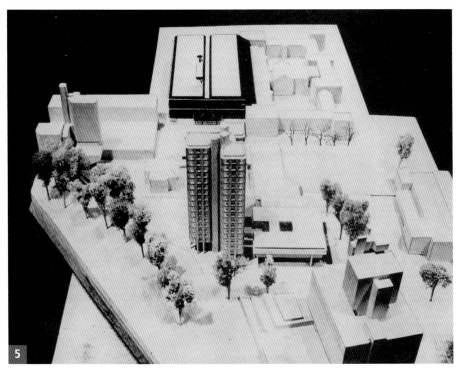

4-9. Interestingly, the 1969 prospectus shows the central campus without the Attenborough Tower; a key feature of the campus since the 1970s, especially since the cleaning of the concrete and replacement of windows in 2008. However, a January 1968 edition of *Ripple* shows an architect's model and plans for developing the Tower alongside other photographs that illustrate the considerable feat of engineering required to build it. The Tower has since become a distinctive feature of the Leicester landscape, although many critical comments have been made over the years about its design. On 30 October 1969 *Ripple* carried an article about the progress of the Tower, following a survey of opinion in which one sociology lecturer said he 'was glad his department was to be kept low down since he was terrified of heights and was certain that the lift would fail to work after a week!'. Many students associate the Attenborough Tower with the paternoster and tell of their adventures on it.

10-13. Over the years many proposals were put forward for the development of the central campus including a new library with air conditioning. Since the 1970s the University had always hoped to redevelop its Library. This ambition was realised in 2005 when the current Vice-Chancellor, Bob Burgess with the Librarian, Christine Fyfe, performed the ground breaking ceremony for this £32 million new development (part of a £300 million Development Plan). Among its many modern features are solar panels and an environmentally-sustainable ventilation system which uses automatic sensors to regulate the building's temperature naturally. The project was completed in 2008 and is clearly a dramatic improvement on the original University Library (now the Law Library), located in the main Fielding Johnson Building, as shown here (13).

14-15. It is very rare for any university to close a building, even temporarily. However, in June 1973, the Bennett Building's Geography Reading Room roof collapsed and the then Vice-Chancellor took immediate action to close the building on the grounds of health and safety. The October edition of *Ripple* reported that the Physics Building also incorporated the same type of roof and this was immediately propped up to enable its continued use.

16. Leicester had wanted a medical school since the 1940s with the case being argued by people from the City and University College. However, it was not until the Todd Report on *Medical Education* was published in 1968 that Leicester got its wish when it was agreed that it should be one of three new medical schools in Britain. Some of the original staff shown in this photograph have served their whole careers in Leicester and have only recently retired from the University.

17-19. One key characteristic of the Medical School is its strong links with the University Hospitals of Leicester NHS Trust. The University has staff working within many UHL departments but it also has its own building on the site of the Leicester Royal Infirmary. The University's Robert Kilpatrick Clinical Sciences Building was completed in the early part of 1978 and has given the added benefit of enabling University of Leicester staff to conduct their research within a hospital setting.

20-21. Links between the disciplines of Medicine and Biological Sciences have also been a key feature of the University since the opening of the Medical School. Collaborative work between these two areas take place through medical departments such as Cardiovascular Sciences, Infection, Immunity and Inflammation and Health Sciences but also through several other departments including Biochemistry, Genetics and Cell Physiology and Pharmacology.

22. The most recent addition to Medicine and Biological Sciences is the Henry Wellcome Biomedical Sciences Building which was opened in 2006 by Dr Mark Walport, Director of the Wellcome Trust. This is a state of the art building located in the same area as the Medical School and contains laboratories that are used by staff and graduate students drawn from several departments in the School of Biological Sciences, thus enabling inter-disciplinary work.

23-28. Leicester's Engineering Building is of great historical and architectural interest. It is a landmark listed building by Stirling and Gowan which has many distinctive features some of which are portrayed in the drawings and photographs shown.

29. A special postage stamp was also issued in 1971 to commemorate the Engineering Building's construction, indicating its national importance. This was part of a set to commemorate modern university buildings.

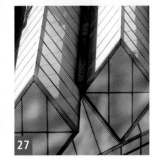

7½2p
University of Leicester

30-31. In April 1998 the Minister for Science, John Battle, officially opened the Space Research Centre. Subsequently, it provided a close connection with the City by linking work undertaken by University academics with work carried out in Leicester's National Space Centre, in which the University was a partner and received funding from the Millennium Commission.

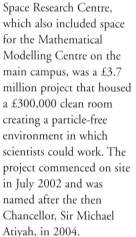

32. The second phase of the Space Research Centre, which also included space for the Mathematical Modelling Centre on the main campus, was a £3.7 million project that housed a £300,000 clean room creating a particle-free environment in which scientists could work. The project commenced on site in July 2002 and was named after the then Chancellor, Sir Michael Atiyah, in 2004.

33. In late 2002 work began to create the new Film Theatre in the Attenborough Seminar Block. This has proved highly successful with the Film Studies students and is also used for a wide range of other activities, including public lectures.

34-35. The University provides many lecture theatres and teaching facilities and, until 2008, perhaps some of the largest and most well-known were within the Ken Edwards Building. Although the building houses the School of Management, University-wide, public and private lectures have regularly been held in its three lecture theatres, all of which are linked. The largest can provide seating for an audience of up to 250.

36. This was surpassed by the lecture theatre within the new David Wilson Library which opened in April 2008 and can accommodate an audience of 500 alongside three breakout rooms. This is an excellent addition to the University's provision and will be an invaluable resource for those wishing to organise large lectures by well-known speakers who are likely to draw a large crowd, such as those given as part of the University's 50th Anniversary celebrations by Professor Stephen Hawking and Professor Sir Alec Jeffreys.

Halls

37-38. In 1958 Leicester built a new Hall of Residence, later to become College Hall. The residents at the time found the disruption rather frustrating. On 1 November 1958 *Ripple* reported that 'Obviously this is the wrong time to be in Women's Hall. Two years from now 183 students will be living in sumptuous surroundings, a very far cry from the austerity and cramped accommodation available in College Hall. The new hall, designed by Sir Leslie Martin, will be started on a site near Knighton Road – a stone's throw from the Cradock public house – within the next month and should be one of the finest of its kind in the country.' The new College Hall was opened in January 1961 by Lady Adrian, the wife of the University's first Chancellor, who had a deep interest in women's education. As with all University accommodation, College Hall subsequently housed both male and female students.

39-43. Unlike, the Knighton Road College Hall development, many of the Oadby Halls, including Beaumont (40), Southmeade (41), Stamford Hall (42) and Highgrove (43), were originally large private houses owned by major industrialists in Leicester. Many of them now form part of the grounds of the magnificent Botanic Gardens and have proved to be a very popular location with students as Halls of Residence.

40

41

42

43

44

44. The particulars of sale for Highgrove indicate the scale of the property which was ideal for student use although the final sale figures for these properties cannot be disclosed! The purchase of these properties was negotiated by the then Registrar, Harold Martin, after whom the Botanic Gardens are named and who undoubtedly secured a good deal for the University.

45-46. As a result of increasing demand, another new type of student accommodation opened at the University of Leicester in 1993 as Putney Road houses, latterly named Nixon Court after Sir Edwin Nixon, a former Chairman of Council. These were built to house the growing number of postgraduate students and those wishing to remain in Leicester during the summer vacation. As reported in the January 1995 *Bulletin*, Phase I opened in the autumn of 1993 with 264 rooms on six floors. Phase II opened in two stages in September and November of 1995 providing an additional eight-storey building of 184 rooms, including 40 en-suite, and a six storey building of 258 rooms and two self-contained flats. A common room and two launderettes were also provided and charges were £40 per week for en-suite facilities, inclusive of heating and light (in 2008 charges for a similar type of room were approximately £85 per week).

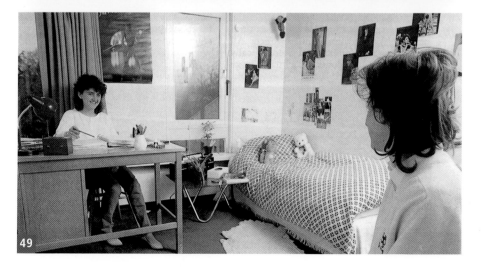

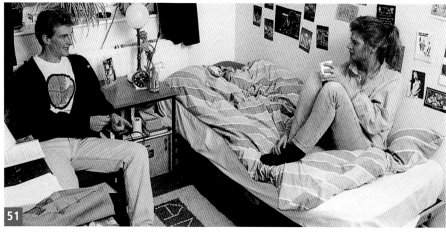

47-51. These pictures give a flavour of the residential facilities available at the University and how they have changed over the years.

52-54. In December 2007, another new Hall of Residence that was, initially, called New Hall was opened in honour of the outgoing Chairman of Council John Foster. It is now the University's largest Hall of Residence, providing accommodation for a total of 581 students in a variety of catered and self-catered rooms. The Hall is an innovative design, styled in pavilions, and its rooms provide an essential requirement for the modern student: en-suite facilities.

Recreational Buildings

55-58. This model shows 'the new Charles Wilson Amenities Building, the Sports Hall seen from above and one of the Refectories in October 1967. Although *Ripple* expressed concern at the 'differences between staff and student facilities [which] are there again, in spite of brave attempts to produce better student-staff relationships with a joint common room. They have a carpet on their refectory floor and a balcony at each corner of it.' Such statements are a reminder of the divisions that once existed between staff and students in universities. The Charles Wilson building was opened by Sir Charles Wilson, the first Vice-Chancellor, on Friday 25 September 1967, and included three refectories, several common rooms, a large coffee bar, a Sports Hall with changing rooms and a weight-training room. Members of the University staff were present at the ceremony and were rewarded with a free sherry!

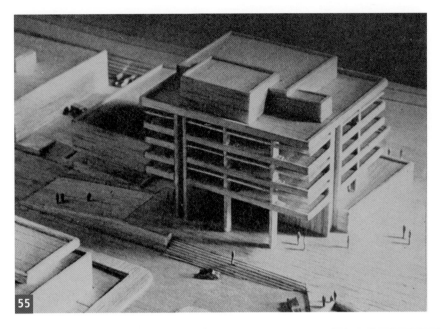

59-63. The Students' Union has been housed in the Percy Gee Building since 1958 and aims to represent students through a wide range of social, cultural, religious and sporting activities. Over the years it has also provided a range of services based upon student demand including a shop, travel advice and bookings, a second-hand bookshop, an optician, print shop and gym as well as a student-focused job centre.

Investment and Refurbishment

64-68. As can be seen from this montage of campus shots, the University has changed considerably over the past fifty years, growing in size and adding new buildings through many investment and refurbishment programmes. However, it still retains its campus feel and the friendly atmosphere of which we are all immensely proud.

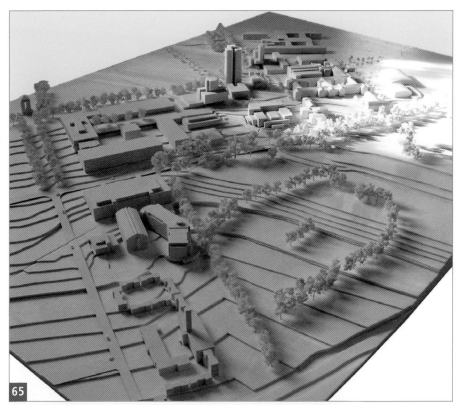

67

North Campus

London Road

Tigers Way

Regents Road

Mandela Park

Regent College

Lancaster Road

De Montfort Hall

Victoria Park

University Road

Welford Road Cemetery

Central Campus

Welford Road

Freemen's Common

Wyggeston and Queen Elizabeth I College

Victoria Park Road

railway

South Campus

Nixon Court

68

The University in 2008

69-70. The University of Leicester is located primarily on two major sites: the academic buildings are only a short distance from the City Centre in and around University Road and the student village and sports facilities are in the residential suburb of Oadby about two miles away. In addition, the University has buildings on each of Leicester's hospital sites: the Royal Infirmary, the Glenfield Hospital and the General Hospital as well as individual properties around the City. 2008: The University of Leicester Main Campus (69), The Oadby Campus, University of Leicester (70).

3. Teaching and Learning

Teaching, learning and assessment are conducted in numerous ways including lectures; laboratory work; fieldwork; seminars; tutorials; independent study; continuous assessment; and, of course, the dreaded examinations! These may be as familiar to students in 2008 as they were in 1958 but it is there that the similarities end. Numerous changes have occurred in teaching methods over the last fifty years, where learning technologists have worked with teachers and researchers to transform the teaching process. In Leicester, the range of subjects always extended across the arts, sciences and social sciences which were joined by some significant disciplinary developments following the expansion of higher education in the 1960s. Among the 'new' subject areas developed in Leicester was Law – established in 1965, with its first intake in 1966 of 36 students that by 2008 had grown to a department of 1,017. Similarly, the School of Medicine was established in 1974, with an intake of 50 students in 1975 that had grown to 1,244 in 2008, with an annual intake of 162 Home/EU students. These trends have been sustained in the 21st century where Leicester has continued to innovate through the introduction of two year Foundation Degrees in subjects such as Educational Studies for Teaching Assistants and Drug and Alcohol Counselling, and new specialised Masters' programmes, including the MA in The Country House and MSc's in Pain Management and Cancer Chemistry, among many others.

The University is also a major provider of distance learning courses, a limited number of which were developed in the 1990s where they were seen as an unusual departure for a research intensive university. However, this development proved highly successful and is now at the heart of the University's mainstream postgraduate provision with approximately one third of students studying in this way. This also facilitated a wider range of new, vocational, Masters courses, predominantly in management and other social sciences, together with some programmes in archaeology and psychology. In 1992 there were 68 distance learning students whereas in 2008 there were 8,902 students registered for such courses. This growth has resulted in the University's two winter Degree Congregations being predominantly for postgraduates (who constituted approximately 50% of the University's total numbers in 2008).

Many of these new programmes arose within new subject areas. The Department of Adult Education spawned the Centre for Mass Communications Research, which has subsequently become the Department of Media and Communication. Similarly, the School of Social Work began within the Department of Adult Education and has become a freestanding subject affiliated to the Medical School. Other areas established out of the Adult Education Department include the Richard Attenborough Centre for Disability and the Arts and the Scarman Centre for Public Order (which became the Department of Criminology). Leicester also pioneered innovative inter-disciplinary curricula through taught Masters programmes in areas such as Museum Studies and Victorian Studies which brought together teaching staff from a range of different subject disciplines either within one department or within a centre with subjects drawn from arts, humanities and the social sciences.

A major characteristic of English higher education has been the focus on developing new degree programmes based on the disciplinary research conducted by academic staff. Inevitably, this led to a focus on the subject, with relatively little consideration being given to teaching styles and the importance of providing high quality teaching. It was not until the 1990s that English higher education institutions had their teaching reviewed by the Quality Assurance Agency which resulted in considerable debate about how such visits should be conducted, although an important consequence was a growing interest in teaching methods and curriculum content. This was reflected in the 2003 White Paper on *The Future of Higher Education* which addressed the question of strengthening and developing teaching so that it took on as much importance as research, with a network of Centres of Excellence in Teaching and Learning (CETLs) being created. Links between research and teaching were now fundamental in all the University's work. Many initiatives were subsequently developed to give teaching greater status, all of which required staff commitment to teaching, learning and research, and were used as an indicator in staff promotions. In order to keep staff up-to-date with teaching developments, many opportunities are provided in Leicester for them to develop both personally and professionally. A number of awards have been obtained by departments and individuals including Investors in People, which demonstrates high standards in business performance, and schemes such as the Higher Education Academy's National Teaching Fellowships, which enable staff to display their talents in teaching, learning and the development of the student experience.

In the national competition to develop CETLs, Leicester led two successful bids: Genetics Education Networking

for Innovation and Excellence (GENIE) and Spatial Literacy in Teaching in Geography (SPLINT) and participated in a third Centre in Physics. These Centres attracted around £4 million of funding which put them on a par with research centres. Interestingly, all three were embedded in departments where the University had considerable research strengths throughout its fifty year history and where staff had an international research reputation. Outreach work through CETLs also provided staff with the opportunity to engage with school pupils and help them participate in a university taster experience. This has become an important area of work for Leicester staff as there is a strongly held belief in the importance of higher education being accessible to those under-represented in universities and Leicester actively encourages mature students and those from disadvantaged backgrounds to enrol on its degree programmes. Short courses and summer schools are also held to improve access and to encourage students to go to University. For example, in Chemistry through its Spectroscopy in a Suitcase programme which is taken into schools to promote the study of science.

Teaching and learning at university also involves a considerable amount of private study, for which not all students are prepared. Schools have begun to recognise this and developed programmes in conjunction with universities to ensure that their students increase self-motivation, develop good organisational skills and engage in independent learning. Leicester has a strong specialist team responsible for schools' liaison who run frequent events for schoolchildren to enable them to gain an understanding of university life and encourage them to consider this as the next step in their educational development. One such event was the lecture run by Dr Raynor and Professor Holloway over a twenty five year period entitled 'Chemistry is Fun'. Many thousands of children in groups from 200 to 2000 attended their lecture in Westminster Hall. Alongside these initiatives, the Colleges-University of Leicester Network (CULN) was established in 2000, involving over twenty further education and sixth form colleges to ease the transition between school/college and university. Student progression is a major aspect of national policy that is implemented through CULN and has resulted in these colleges becoming greater providers of the University's undergraduate students.

Not only has the way in which students are introduced to university life changed, so have their expectations of how they will be taught and assessed. The move from using the blackboard to communicating through blogs is now commonplace but universities remain very traditional in their methods of assessment. For example, class essays were predominantly handwritten in the 1950s and 1960s (and rarely used for assessment, which took the form of timed examinations). Subsequently, some students used portable typewriters to produce class essays up until the 1980s, by which time essays were being used to count towards assessment for the final degree. In 2008 it is a requirement that all assessed work is word-processed, although timed examinations remain handwritten and both modes of assessment count towards the final result. The Queen's Hall will therefore be as familiar to students of the 1950s as it is to students today, being the place where traditional examinations are held. Nevertheless, at least today's students get a degree certificate whereas, until 1966 Leicester students received no formal certificate! Qualifications, certificates and modes of assessment have all been on the higher education agenda over the years. By 2008, there was a growing national debate about the ways in which students were examined, their degrees classified and transcripts used to provide a more comprehensive record of student achievement.

Among the reasons for these developments are demands from employers for further information on student performance. Ensuring that students in the 21st century leave university with a good degree is only the start. In a highly competitive world there needs to be an element of 'value added' which is demonstrated by innovations such as the Leicester Award for Employability Skills. Initially endorsed by the Institute of Leadership and Management, this Award enabled Leicester's students to gain maximum value and increase their employability skills through work experience, part-time work, volunteering and extra-curricular commitments. Students attended workshops, completed work-based assignments and an oral presentation, covering topics expected of good employees including teamwork, leadership, presentation skills, personal development, business skills and problem solving.

While academic staff are important in delivering degree programmes, all university courses and additional programmes require assistance from support staff including those in student welfare, careers, learning technology and the library. Leicester's David Wilson Library gives students access to a range of dedicated information professionals as well as much of the material they may require, be it in hard copy or electronic format. University libraries have traditionally provided books and journals for consultation but these have undergone a major transformation over the years as contemporary students have access to a wider range of material through electronic books and journals and online sources. One could say that there is now no need for a student to visit the library as more material is provided electronically but much of this is only available through library subscriptions. The library therefore remains a necessary resource as well as providing students with a central location for quiet study. Consequently, it is important for universities to continue developing their facilities and courses to meet demand whilst appointing high quality scholars who are passionate about their teaching and research and can encourage the development of tomorrow's researchers. The changes over the last fifty years have been immense and we hope to have captured the fact that Leicester has developed a synergy between high quality teaching and research and that there is also a light-hearted aspect to learning which is not just about hard work.

Lectures, Demonstrations, Tutorials and Practicals

1. An example of a typical classroom situation in the late 1980s with Professor Roy Davies (Pure Mathematics) engaged in small group teaching in Mathematics. Professor Davies is using the traditional method of teaching with a blackboard which, in today's teaching environment, has different connotations (as demonstrated by photograph 40 in this chapter).

2. In addition to classroom work, teaching and learning takes many other forms, including large lectures, demonstrations and practical work. Lectures involve the use of a variety of illustrations through handouts, books, film and more recently video and PowerPoint. Here, for example, Dr J Barrie Raynor of the Chemistry Department is carrying out a demonstration. He is illustrating spontaneous combustion by placing a small amount of phosphorus in a container which is filled with oxygen and igniting it with the tip of a heated metal rod. As can be seen, this burns with a bright light and, we are told, gives out very little heat.

3. Many courses provide an opportunity for students to engage in hands-on experience, which takes a variety of forms. These include enabling students to understand the practical application of their studies by working in small groups. This class of Applied Mathematics students in the early 1990s, for example, are engaged in an investigation into forces and gravity.

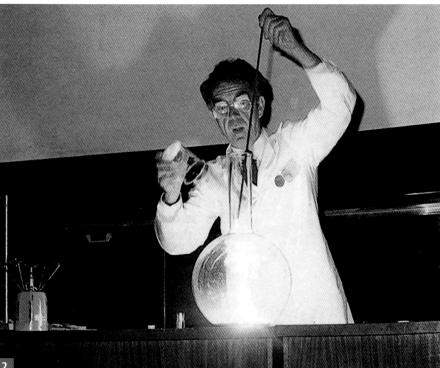

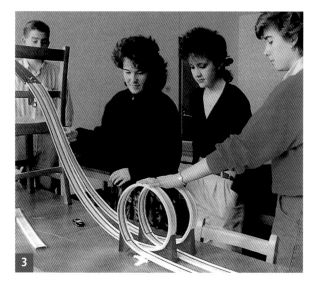

4. The University offers many courses in vocational areas: museum studies, law, labour market studies and medicine. Leicester's Medical School works in collaboration with many local teaching hospitals. An essential component in the training of doctors is bedside teaching which is conducted by academic staff and hospital consultants. This group of students from the late 1980s is being taught by the distinguished founding Professor of Surgery Peter Bell (who was subsequently knighted for his outstanding contribution to the field of medicine) shown discussing the results of an abdominal x-ray with a patient.

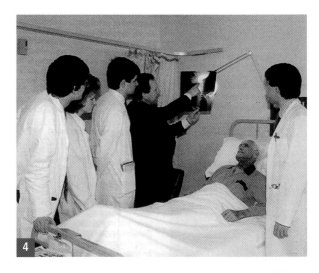

5. Tutorials are a key component in the delivery of the undergraduate curriculum. Departments, and in turn tutors, organise tutorials (or classes) in many different ways. This group of Economics students, for example, is being advised by Derek Deadman in a statistics class in the mid-1970s. They are using an electric desktop calculator, which was considered to be state-of-the-art equipment. These machines preceded the widespread use of hand-held calculators in the Department by a few years and PCs by about a decade. It was thought to be important at the time that the machines had a paper roll on the top which kept a record of, and printed out, the student's calculations and in examinations, students had to hand in their roll stapled to their scripts so that they could receive marks for their working. There was also a bell on the machine which rang if students attempted to carry out calculations that caused memory overflow which caused considerable noise during examinations!

6. A hallmark of teaching in research-intensive universities, such as Leicester, is that students are taught by researchers at the leading-edge of their subject. Many lecturers are therefore well-known nationally in their fields and through the media. For example, Julian Boon is a distinguished forensic psychologist who has assisted police forces throughout the country with psychological profiling and has presented many television programmes alongside his teaching in Leicester.

7. Modern language teaching provides an opportunity for students to speak and write fluently in their chosen language. They are also able to read and discuss the country's literature, history, politics and culture in small groups, as illustrated by this group of students studying German in the early 1990s.

Independent Study

8

8. While a considerable amount of teaching is conducted within formal settings, a distinctive feature of a University education is the ability to engage in independent study. Much of this is carried out in departmental libraries across the campus as well as in the main University Library. Law students, for example, have access to major resources in the Harry Peach Library (which, until 1974, was the original Main Library).

9. The School of Education's specialist library of books and curriculum materials provided many of the essential resources to assist PGCE (Postgraduate Certificate of Education) students in lesson planning and preparation, using the resources likely to be available within local schools in which teaching practice occurred.

10. Distance learning at graduate level is an area in which Leicester (after the Open University) leads the field and is another example where students engage in independent study. In 2008 there were nearly 9,000 Leicester students studying by distance learning throughout the world. The University offers high-quality flexible, supported study at postgraduate level.

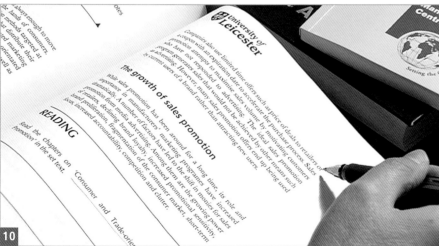

10

9

Lab Work

11. Students choose their courses for a variety of reasons. Nicole McGrath, a third year Medical Biochemistry student (in 2006), commented "I decided to come to Leicester really because of the Department's excellent reputation that I had heard about from teachers at my college. I am absolutely loving the degree. I really enjoy the lab-work and being hands-on – putting the theory into practise – it's brilliant." Nicole subsequently registered on the MBChB degree at Leicester.

12. Lab work is also an integral part of many degrees in the physical and life sciences. In 2003 the Chemistry laboratories underwent extensive refurbishment to provide state-of-the-art facilities for teaching as well as research. This work is supervised by tutors including Paul Jenkins, shown here with Fiona Saunders (right) and Gemma Smith (left) who graduated in 2006. Fiona commented "I enjoy the forensic science modules. The lab facilities are excellent and there is a wide range of experiments to conduct".

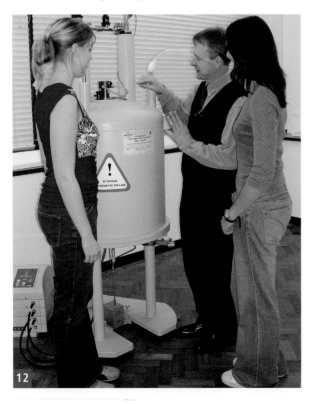

Fieldwork

ARE FIELD COURSES ALL WORK AND FOOT SORES?

Urban studies in Torremelinos.

Goat on a stick.

Do you want to come up and look at my overthrusting?

The Geography Department Fieldwork Course to Spain 1975, was in all respects an amazing seven days. Urban development and Geological structure were the subjects, and some work even got done. The rest of the time was spent on a coach, climbing mountains, or in "El Bier Keller". Anyway, even if you couldn't give a damn about Spain, I hope you like the photographs.

EL TIGRE.

Raquel Welch? Who's she?

I'm amazed, truly amazed!

El group photograph.

I wonder what the weather's like in Leicester.

And so to bed...

I told you the hotal wouldn't be ready!

14

13. In many subjects, Leicester students have the opportunity to conduct fieldwork, using a range of techniques in a variety of settings. All Archaeology students, for example, are required to do at least eight weeks' excavation or field survey in the vacations during their three years. As suggested by this photograph taken in the early 1990s, digs take place in many locations in this country and abroad. In 2006 students and staff engaged in a project through University of Leicester Archaeological Services (ULAS) that saw large areas of Leicester city centre excavated in advance of the building of the new Highcross shopping complex.

14. The student perspective adds a new dimension to what it means to study for a degree and what additional activities are involved within and beyond the classroom. In May 1975, *Ripple* carried a record of a Geography field course that had taken place at Easter. This demonstrated that there is a light-hearted side to teaching and learning and all the hard work! Indeed, we are told that many field courses in Geography were booked as package deals to reduce the cost which, if the students had been told, might have suggested that they were going on holiday.

13

Examinations

15. Continuous assessment is a method used more widely in recent years to examine students' work. Most Masters programmes in the University are examined exclusively by coursework and dissertation where students receive feedback that can be used to develop their work, as on this assessed essay.

16. Many graduates will recall formal examinations as part of their time at Leicester. The examination hall in the Percy Gee Building is an all-too-familiar aspect of university life.

Brown, Jane The Pursuit of Paradise a social history of gardens and gardening (London Harper Collins, 1999)

For the student of landscape gardens in relation to the English country house this is a particularly interesting book as it covers a wider range of social history and its affect on garden design It also focuses on pleasure and secret gardens, literature (for example how Beatrix Potter wrote her books in code), the development of the ha-ha and so on It is a book that may appear to be rather less academic or theoretical than some cited but actually provides good information from a social historical perspective. *Does it have any kind of scholarly approach which could be used for further research?*

Clark, H F The English Landscape Garden (Gloucester Alan Sutton Publishing Limited, 1980).

Clark starts by giving a clear summary of the topic and then concentrates on particular gardens,

15

16

Opportunities for Students

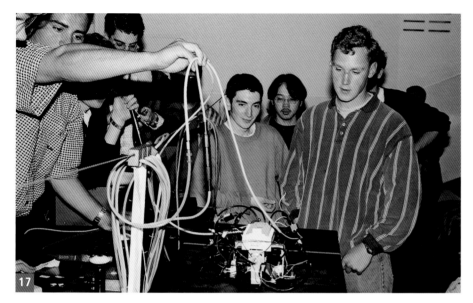

17. During their time at Leicester, many students have the opportunity to take part in competitions within and beyond the University. The Robot Olympics has become an annual event within the Engineering Department where students are invited to develop a robot to carry out a particular task using specific materials. For example, in 1997 a total of 120 students took part in this event. Student Tom Harrison, one of the competitors, said "Eight robots were entered into the race which involved a flat sprint as well as climbing up inclines. The fastest sprint time was 23 seconds for covering a distance of nine feet, while one robot almost managed a sheer face climb. Many different types of robot were produced from a multi-legged caterpillar design to a hovercraft creation utilising a bicycle pump. The day was great fun and the majority of the Engineering Department were there cheering loudly."

18. Some courses, such as Engineering, offer an opportunity for students to undertake work placements arranged by the department with local, regional and national companies as part of their degree course. Nick Mills, for example, spent a placement year working with Thames Water and, after graduating in Electrical and Electronic Engineering in 2005, was able to secure permanent employment with this company as a Project Engineer.

19. This poster was produced by Leicester's Law students following their third successive win in four years in the 1974 Observer Mooting Competition.

20. The Leicester Award for Employability Skills, endorsed by the Institute of Leadership and Management, was introduced in 2006 as an additional means of demonstrating a student's potential to future employers. Claire Newport, a 3rd year Psychology student, was presented with an award of distinction in recognition of her outstanding performance in 2007. Claire was a highly motivated student who engaged fully with the Leicester Award and achieved the highest marks for her assignments. She used her experience as a telephone helpline volunteer with the Eating Disorder Association (EDA) in her first assignment, which was highly commended by Leicester Award tutors. Claire commented that the Leicester Award had been 'one of the best and most productive learning experiences that I have had during my time at Leicester University'.

21. 'Languages at Leicester' is the University's programme of language courses for non-specialists. It offers short courses in up to 12 languages, from beginners upwards in French, German, Italian, Spanish, Russian, Arabic, Chinese, Dutch, Polish, Greek, Japanese and Portuguese.

22. 'International Student Awards' is a prestigious award scheme run by the British Council. The competition recognises international students whose proactive approach to life overseas, away from their homes and families, is enhancing their personal development. Students are asked to write a letter home, explaining how they are making the most of their time in the UK. Leicester students Than Htut from Myanmar (studying for an MSc in Educational Leadership) and Li-ying Lin from Taiwan (studying Medicine) were selected as regional runner-up prize winners in the 2007 International Student Awards. The East Midlands Development Agency, one of nine Regional Development Agencies in England, also supported the 2007 awards by presenting trophies to the best entries from colleges and universities in the East Midlands region. Li-Ying and Than were presented with their trophies in a ceremony at the University of Leicester on 17 April 2007.

Future Careers

23. A very different approach to graduate recruitment was clearly illustrated in an open letter to graduates placed as an advertisement in *Ripple* in December 1960, when Air Marshal Sir Arthur McDonald wrote to encourage 'men' to consider the Royal Air Force as a career.

24. Leicester has an excellent record for its students gaining graduate employment following their studies and many students go on to successful careers in industry. For example, Choo Beng Khoo, who studied Mechanical Engineering and graduated with an upper second class honours degree in 1999. He was employed with Sarawak Shell Berhad as Operations Engineer from 2001-2003 as the Platform Supervisor and subsequently became Project Operations Engineer for Shell Asia Pacific.

25. Being able to access advice on the world of work is vital for students. Careers education is provided through discussions with tutors in departments as well as with the team of professionals within Leicester's Student Support Service. A regular feature of Careers Education is the annual Employment Fair, where over 80 employers visit the University to discuss future prospects with students. These fairs were also very successfully organised by students as well as by the Careers Service.

Adult Education and Lifelong Learning

26-27. A variety of short courses and certificate programmes in the arts and humanities are available to many people within Leicester, Leicestershire and Rutland through the University's Lifelong Learning provision (previously Adult Education). A very popular group of courses are those involving art and drawing classes which are provided for a range of students, including those with disabilities. This blind student is being taught in the University studio in the early 1990s. Such courses now take place in the Richard Attenborough Centre for Disability and the Arts.

28. Adult education has a long history in Leicester with University courses being provided through the facilities at Vaughan College located in the city centre. In 2001 the art of tai-chi, which was taught at Vaughan College, was demonstrated in the adjacent Castle Gardens as part of Adult Learners' Week.

Staff Development

29

29-30. High-quality teaching has now been recognised nationally through the introduction of the National Teaching Fellowship Scheme. Within many universities various Teaching Award Schemes have also been established and Leicester is no exception. The first teaching awards were made in 2003 to Heather Crick, Pre-Clinical Sciences; Nick Everett, English; Chris Willmott, Biochemistry; and Emma Parker, English (29). Subsequently, Chris Willmott was awarded a National Teaching Fellowship, one of only 50 such awards given annually. In 2008, Professor Annette Cashmore (30) received Leicester's fifth National Teaching Fellowship.

31. Staff are one of the University's most valuable resources and it is important that they are given opportunities for personal and professional development. The Staff Development Centre provides many courses, often taught by colleagues. In 1994, training sessions were provided on a Skills Transfer programme where technicians with skills and experience in one area could pass on their knowledge to technicians in other disciplines. Shown here are members of the Central Photographic Unit providing a course on darkroom techniques for staff on the first Skills Transfer Course.

31

30

The Students of Tomorrow

32. The University also offers the opportunity for the students of tomorrow to experience its facilities, to encourage them to consider a university career. In April 1999, eight departments ran taster courses for 268 Leicestershire sixth-form students. Among the departments participating was Archaeology where students had an opportunity to study bones excavated from dig sites.

33. Providing for young people who would otherwise not have access to facilities is of paramount importance to the University. In the mid-1990s Leicester was successful in leading a project to establish the National Space Science Centre. It included the development of a Challenger Learning Centre which provides an opportunity for children to work on scientific projects through space simulations.

34. Schoolchildren are also given the opportunity at the Department of Physics' annual Space School to experience weightlessness through scuba diving.

35. At the start of the 21st century the University won a major competition to establish innovative centres in Teaching and Learning (Centres of Excellence in Teaching and Learning). One CETL is called GENIE (Genetics Education Networking for Innovation and Excellence) and is located within the Department of Genetics. Among its many activities is work with local schools to introduce pupils to scientific activities. Suzanne Lavelle, a PhD student in the Genetics Department, seen here working with two pupils from Ibstock Community College building DNA models at a Dynamic DNA event in September 2006. This was a hands-on event for three hundred 14-15 year olds from Leicestershire schools to celebrate the opening of the GENIE outreach laboratories in the Medical Sciences Building.

36. Another HEFCE funded CETL is called SPLINT (Spatial Literacy in Teaching), which is a £3.9 million Centre led by Leicester in conjunction with the University of Nottingham and University College London. The focus of SPLINT is on the teaching of geospatial technologies; taught postgraduate courses; and the enhancement of spatial literacy in higher education.

Changing Teaching Styles

37. Among the many teaching initiatives to have taken place in higher education is computer-based learning. The Economics Department was a contributor to a national project for the development of interactive computer-based learning materials in economics (WinEcon) which provided flexibility in teaching in the late 1990s.

38-39. Two photographs from the Physics and Astronomy Department in 1990 (38) and 2006 (39) which illustrates advances in modern technology and teaching environments.

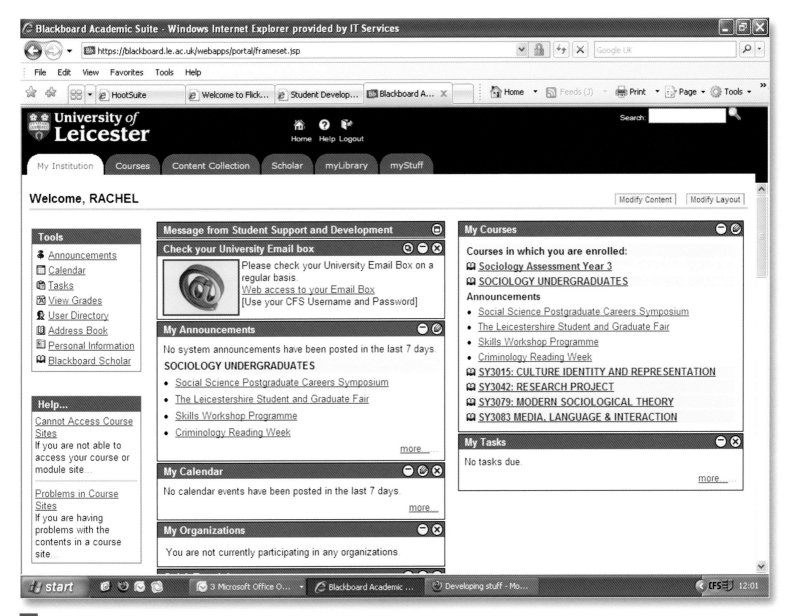

40. Technology has revolutionised teaching methods and has led to the establishment of virtual learning environments including 'Blackboard' – an integrated environment enabling online communication between students and tutors. Course material is published on a course website with online classes and automatic marking.

41. At Leicester, technological development led to the appointment of Gilly Salmon (pictured left) as the University's Professor of E-Learning and Learning Technologies who established the Beyond Distance Research Alliance. This promotes e-learning, facilitates research and development into information, communication and learning technologies, provides the opportunity for networking and collaboration and the development of strategies for curriculum development. One initiative is the Media Zoo (in which this photograph is taken) which provides staff with a supportive environment in which to develop an understanding of the design of learning activities using learning technologies, such as iPods and blogs.

42. One of thirteen group study rooms in the David Wilson Library. These are rooms which only students can book and which are equipped with a wall mounted plasma screen and PC which helps to promote group learning.

4. Research

Research is at the heart of a university and is a key feature in distinguishing it from schools and colleges. It has been true of the University of Leicester since it began. Most of the teaching staff within the University are leading researchers as well as teachers who contribute to the advancement of their disciplines and regularly produce books, journal articles and conference papers that contribute to society's knowledge base and move their disciplines forward. In some cases, academic staff find themselves contributing to major discoveries that have a dramatic impact worldwide.

Since the establishment of the University, Leicester has been the home of many discoveries and academic developments arising from research projects in a range of departments. However, it is a daunting task to give more than a flavour of the University's research, especially in a non-technical way. We have therefore selected just a few illustrations to highlight the different kinds of research in which the University is involved. A major discovery in Leicester was DNA Fingerprinting by Professor Sir Alec Jeffreys in his Genetics Laboratory in 1984, from which he still works. This has had a massive and revolutionary impact on many fields of enquiry on a global scale.

Over the last fifty years, the Department of Physics and Astronomy has had a very distinguished research record, leading the field nationally and internationally through its involvement in numerous space programmes. In research evaluations, the Department has been highly rated and its work considered to be of

international standing. It was awarded the Queen's Anniversary Prize for Higher Education in 1994. The Department is renowned for its major research programmes in condensed matter physics, space science and astrophysics and has been recognised as a leading international centre for X-ray Astronomy. The University has also had a piece of equipment operating in orbit every year since 1967.

Inter-disciplinary activities have always been a feature of work in Leicester and the Physics and Astronomy Department has therefore fostered close relationships with other departments. Working with such diverse subjects as Chemistry, Engineering and Medicine it has been involved in studies of nanoparticles in the targeted treatment of cancers, damage to DNA by airborne particles and new magnetic materials for high data storage. In 1998 the University Space Research Centre was opened to enable the Department to further develop instrumentation for a range of new space missions involving collaborations with the European Space Agency, NASA, India, China, and Russia. Leicester also has a number of successful spin-out companies including Bio-Astral which uses space techniques for bio-medical applications.

Research is conducted in many other scientific areas where links are made to industrial development. For example, the development of new drugs, vaccines, plant tolerance and disease reduction offer potential benefits to the medical and agricultural industries through the Department of Chemistry's work on anti-cancer agents and Plant Biology's development of lead tolerance.

The past fifty years has also seen a diverse range of major international collaborative research programmes and individual research projects across many departments, including Geology. These have enabled Leicester geologists to make a significant contribution across geoscience by increasing their understanding of how the earth works. Geology in Leicester is synonymous with the name of Peter Sylvester-Bradley who led the Department for almost twenty years from 1958. He was responsible for many developments including the introduction of economic geology, the expansion in geophysics (using physical principles to study properties of the earth) and crustal evolution alongside major research programmes in East Africa and Central Asia which are still important in 2008. Among the specialist research fields developed by the Department are palaeobiology (the study of ancient organisms), sedimentology (the study of the sequence of deposits and the processes that cause the formation of those deposits making up the uppermost part of the earth's crust) and tectonics (dealing with structures in the earth's crust, and their movement) and petrophysics (the study of the physical and chemical properties that describe the occurrence and behaviour of rocks, soils and fluids). Some of the most exciting research outputs have included the discovery and recognition in Leicestershire of Charnia, one of the earliest known complex fossils, and work on ostracod shells developed by Peter Sylvester-Bradley and David Siveter has resulted in high profile publications in *Nature*, *Science* and the *Proceedings of the Royal Society*. International research on the East African Rift System and a programme of ocean drilling have also been in place since the 1980s; these developments have all influenced the teaching programme.

Another research-intensive area of activity is Archaeology and Ancient History. Begun in 1957, this has benefited the City, the County and the wider East Midlands region. Staff have also been involved in field projects across Britain, Europe, the Mediterranean and beyond. The School has always focused primarily on Landscape Studies, Archaeologies of Historical Periods and Material Culture and Representation. In 1967 Charles Thomas was appointed as the first Professor of Archaeology and under his leadership, and that of subsequent Professors, the department successfully developed its research portfolio on Romano-British towns, British Pre-history and Environmental Archaeology. Further major developments took place after the appointment of Graeme Barker to the Chair of Archaeology in the late 1980s when new research projects and initiatives were developed. The research focus of the Department has also been echoed in appointments and research awards including a Leverhulme Special Research Fellowship for Mark Gillings who joined David Mattingley and Graeme Barker to work on a European research project. Other significant research has been carried out on topics including agriculture and rural life, Cicolano Castles, British landscape history and the British Iron Age.

The School of Archaeology and Ancient History also has an independent professional unit, the University of Leicester Archaeological Services (ULAS), that works across the country on a wide range of projects and also contributes to undergraduate and postgraduate courses on Professional Skills and the Organisation and Management of Archaeology in Britain. Its staff regularly present talks and open days to interested local groups; the unit has particular expertise in urban archaeology which enables development to take place whilst limiting local impact. Projects have included assessment and mitigation for major developments, consultancy and contracting services for developers, including the Highways Agency, the Environment Agency, East Midlands Airport, Severn Trent Water, Hammersons (who were the developers for Leicester's new Highcross Shopping Centre that opened in 2008) and many more. ULAS is a major contributor to the University's links with business and industry and was the top unit in 2008 for Business Quality Research in Leicester.

Many other areas of the University have international reputations such as the Department of Geography; one of the initial subjects developed in University College. Whilst the Department's early focus was on teaching, research began to be developed by Professor Pat Bryan and his small team in 1922 undertaking research in cartography, the American landscape and environmentalism. Research activity was subsequently expanded under the leadership of Professor Norman Pye who contributed to, and facilitated, the development of major research contributions in a range of areas including glacial geomorphology (glacial landforms), marine cartography, pollen analysis, behavioural geography, and landscape analysis. One of the major areas for which Leicester geographers are known is Geographical Information Systems. This emerged in the late 1980s with advances in computer technology when the Department also won grants of over £0.5 million to establish the Midlands Regional Research Laboratory – a centre of excellence for the assembly, manipulation and display of map and statistical data. This initiative was supported by the Social Science Research Council (subsequently the Economic and Social Research Council) and provided opportunities for other external funding and links with companies.

Staff and students in the Department of Engineering have been involved in many local and national research initiatives over the years. In particular, relationships have been developed with a number of major companies such as Jaguar where students undertake research to improve product development. Industrial placements, such as those at Triumph Motorcyles, are also a popular feature of the engineering course which gives students the opportunity to experience their subject in real-life situations and many of these companies regularly sponsor research projects to evaluate key areas of development for society.

Another area conducting highly important research of benefit to the wider community is the Department of Infection, Inflammation and Immunity which investigates issues such as tuberculosis, superbug-resistant drugs, ulcer diagnosis, child health and respiratory medicine and, as in many other Departments, staff here are leaders in their field.

However, Leicester is not just a science-based University, although these areas are often considered to be more photogenic than work in the arts and the social sciences, hence the predominance of scientific photographs. Nevertheless, Leicester also has an excellent reputation in disciplines within arts and social science including English, sociology and law. For example, the English Department has been evaluated as having internationally-renowned researchers and was placed top in the National Student Survey in 2005/06 and 2006/07. Many major sociologists have trained and worked in Leicester including Tony Giddens, John Goldthorpe, Martin Albrow, Joe Banks and Olive Banks, who was Leicester's first woman Professor, appointed in 1974. Ilya Neustadt and Norbert Elias also had a profound influence on the development of the subject nationally and internationally as well as in the Department at Leicester. They trained generations of sociologists who went on to develop the subject in other universities including Richard Brown (at Durham), Sheila Allen (in Bradford) and Dick Scase (at the University of Kent). Some Leicester undergraduates subsequently joined the Departmental staff including Eric Dunning, Terry Johnson and Geoff Hurd. Leicester sociologists have made major contributions to social theory, socio-historical studies and empirical research on such diverse topics as youth training, the professions and football hooliganism.

The smallest Department in the University is History of Art and Film, which has focused its research on British art and Renaissance art and, in Film Studies, British cinema. These specialisms have been represented in the work of the Professors in the Department with Luke Herrmann and Alison Yarrington focusing on British art, while David Ekserdjian has published on Renaissance art including a volume on Correggio. Among the most distinguished former members of the Department was Philip Conisbee who went on to be curator of a number of US museums and galleries including the Museum of Fine Arts, Boston; the Los Angeles County Museum of Art; and the National Gallery of Art in Washington where he was Senior Curator of European Paintings.

By contrast, one of the larger Departments in the University is the School of Law which was established in 1965. Like many Departments at the time, Law focused on providing high quality teaching, research and scholarship. There was a close relationship between teaching and research with the latter not only advancing knowledge of the law but also enriching the teaching programme. The Department currently focuses on a range of approaches to the study of law including doctrinal research, socio-legal research, interdisciplinary work and theoretical approaches. It has two research centres in the fields of European Law and Integration and Utility Consumer Law.

This Chapter highlights some of the research that has been undertaken in the University since 1958 and which will continue well into, and beyond, the 21st century. Leicester also has considerable strengths across a wide range of disciplines from medicine and biology to history and museum studies, as illustrated by the photographs. To support all this research activity the University provides extensive laboratories, a range of departmental libraries and research centres and a state-of-the-art Library. All together these facilities provide the research infrastructure for the development of new ideas and new work which takes the University forward and increases its national and international reputation as a leader in a wide range of fields.

Research and Publications

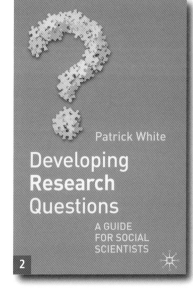

1. A montage of fossils from the Department of Geology, articles about which have been published in *Nature*, *Science* and the *Proceedings of the Royal Society* over the last few years.

2. As well as publishing articles in professional journals, many academic staff have contributed to their discipline by producing monographs and textbooks that draw on research evidence. In the Department of Sociology, Patrick White published a volume in 2008 about doing research and how to establish and develop research questions in the social sciences. It draws on his own experience as a researcher.

3. One of the telescopes at the Astronomy Department (subsequently Physics and Astronomy) at Oadby in the early 1970s. This telescope has now been replaced by a twenty inch reflector that can be used robotically in the same way as one in Majorca used by I-science students.

Physics and Astronomy Research

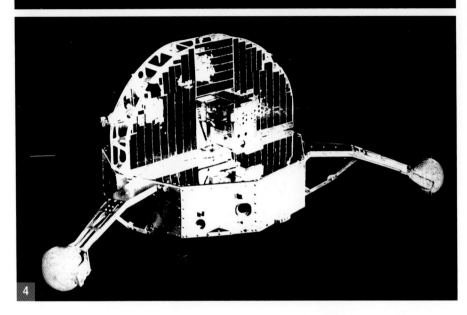

The Sky Is Not The Limit

4. The Department of Physics has developed equipment and experiments for a range of rocket launchings in Europe and the USA since 1967. The launch of a satellite from Cape Kennedy, USA, was front-page news in the 2 November 1967 edition of the student newspaper, *Ripple*. This NASA Orbiting Solar Observatory carried Leicester x-ray detectors to study the sun's radiation and its effects on the upper atmosphere.

5. Work in the Department of Physics has involved developing techniques for studying stars and galaxies that can be used to help in the battle against cancer. This detector was developed in the 1990s to record x-ray emissions for the analysis of human tissue which could impact on the investigation of cancer treating drugs.

6. The rapid development of space research has resulted in a continual demand for more laboratory space and new buildings such as the Space Research Centre. This building has already been extended and, in 2008, a further, third, phase was being considered to accommodate the increased research activity.

7. Large-scale developments in many subject areas involve major investments from a range of sources. Universities have needed to form consortia to bid for the large scale funding required. This wide-field camera, built by a UK consortium led by Leicester, was mounted on the German/UK/US Roentgen Satellite (ROSAT) during pre-flight ground testing in Germany. This experiment conducted the very first survey of the sky in the Extreme Ultraviolet region of the spectrum. It is being examined by former astronaut Honorary Professor Jeff Hoffman. In 1999 a consortium of 18 universities, including Leicester, were successful in establishing funding to develop a four metre telescope known as VISTA (Visible and Infra-red Survey Telescope for Astronomy) that was sited in the Chilean Andes to produce 'atlases' of the sky.

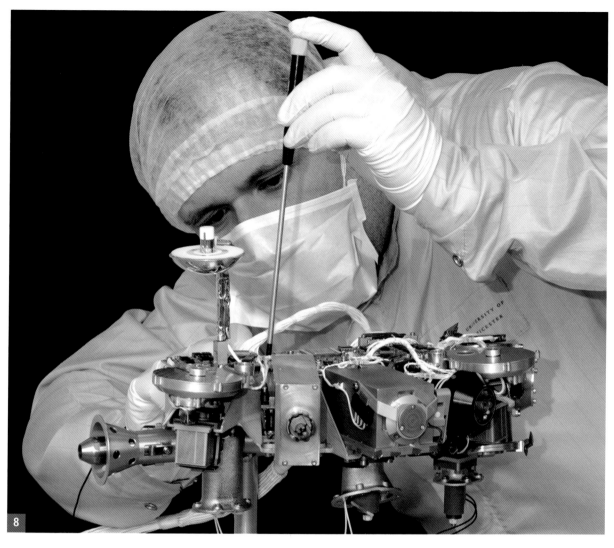

8

8-10. A major space project in 2003 was the first European Mars lander, Beagle 2 flight to Mars, which was due to land on Mars on Christmas Day. This project, involving extensive preparatory work with colleagues from the Open University, entailed a small piece of equipment, weighing just 30kg, being parachuted down to the surface of Mars, along with 9kg of instruments and tools, to search for signs of life. The crucial signal was never received and the equipment never found but our scientists learned many lessons from this mission.

10

9

A Sample of Pure and Applied Research

11

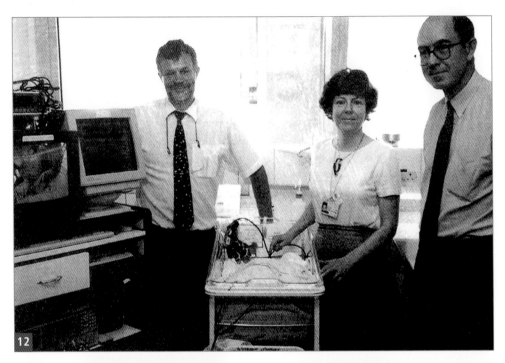

12

11. The University has a number of Research Centres that bring together leading researchers to focus on particular research areas. The Law Department has a number of these centres including the Centre for European Law and Integration (CELI – shown here by its logo) which engages in research and holds seminars and conferences on all aspects of this field.

12. Medical Physics is located at the Leicester Royal Infirmary and is part of the Department of Cardiovascular Science. Researchers have developed innovative blood pressure monitors that are used to improve the monitoring of premature babies.

13. Research on motion sickness in the Department of Psychology was conducted by Jim Reason in the 1970s. He subsequently became a Professor at Manchester University. The person seated in the chair is Bill Williamson who held the equivalent position of today's computer officer in the Department.

14. Psychological research in Leicester covers many areas including work on children, music, human reasoning and judgement. A student is shown studying the psychology of reading development with children at a local primary school.

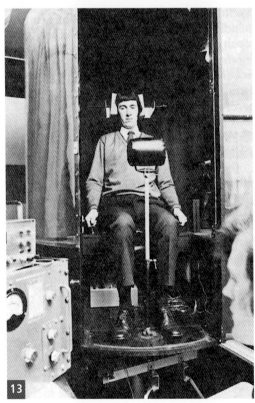

13

14

Some Examples from Engineering

15. Analysing the frequency and response of filters in a sound to light unit during a project supervised by John Fothergill in Engineering which aimed to develop flashing lights for a disco that kept time with the music.

16. Students studying wind effects around a building using a scale model of the Engineering Building in a wind tunnel and with a smoke generator for flow visualisation.

17. Research in engineering brings together theory and practice with a multi-disciplinary approach as well as specific skills in areas such as electronics. An undergraduate student project established in conjunction with Triumph Motorcycles resulted in the student being based on an industrial placement. This project aimed to develop an electrically powered motorbike for entry into an international electrically powered motorbike race. Leicester's bike was the fastest, reaching speeds of up to 90 mph around the circuit at Bruntingthorpe. However, it was also the heaviest as it was based on a Triumph Speed Triple 750 machine donated by Triumph.

18. A significant group in the Department of Engineering is concerned with control systems research which has been involved in developing major technologies such as this experimental helicopter. Many research links have been established with some of the UK's leading aerospace companies such as BAe, Westland and Rolls-Royce.

19. Engineering research has applications in commercial areas and a range of other settings, including developing countries. For example, research into the use of naturally occurring materials in order to provide safe drinking water.

20-21. The Department of Engineering working with Dymag Racing UK Ltd sponsored projects evaluating the strength and composition used in racing wheel manufacture. The Department engaged in fatigue tests on specimens taken from magnesium alloy racing wheels.

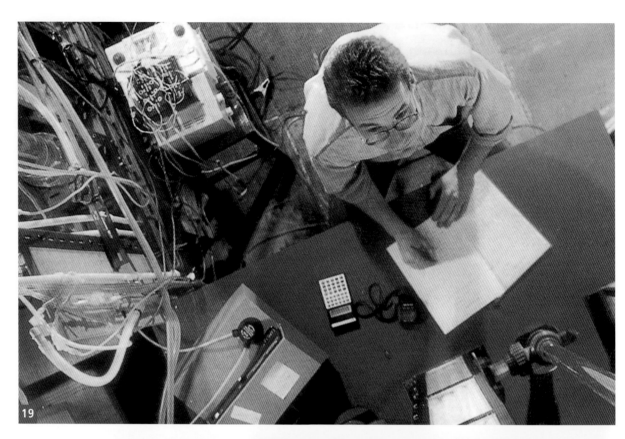

Staff and Student Research Awards

22. A research project in inorganic chemistry being conducted by Robert Lawson, a single subject Chemistry graduate from July 1988 shown using an all-metal vacuum line (necessary for the safe handling of highly reactive fluorine compounds and one of only a few remaining in the UK) for the transfer of a volatile compound into a U-tube cooled in liquid nitrogen.

23. Fundamental scientific research, allied to medicine, is conducted in a range of departments. In the Department of Chemistry, where cancer chemistry is a specialist area of research, work is being carried out to provide a synthetic version of the anti-cancer agent taxol using yew tree clippings.

24. A third-year project student investigating lead-tolerance in various plant species including grasses, in the Department of Botany's laboratories in the 1970s.

25. Many researchers win awards for their work. Arwen Raddon, a Lecturer in the Centre for Labour Market Studies, won a Newer Research Award from the Society for Research in Higher Education in 2005. She used the funding for further research into the development of academic careers.

26. Many academics in the University supervise postgraduate research students who are registered for the degree of PhD and for professional doctorates including the DClinPsy, the DSocSci and the EdD. Clive Dimmock supervised Martha Lam's EdD thesis entitled 'Senior Women Academics in Hong Kong: a Life History Approach'. This was awarded the Ray Bolam Doctoral Thesis Award in 2008 for an important contribution to educational leadership as the judges considered it to be an 'outstanding contribution not only to the field of female gender and management but also to theories of career development linked to notions of identity and socialisation'. She was also complimented on her use of theory development and methodological innovation.

Research Discoveries

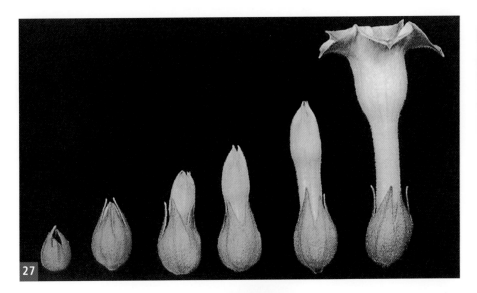

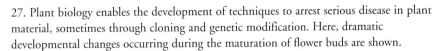

27. Plant biology enables the development of techniques to arrest serious disease in plant material, sometimes through cloning and genetic modification. Here, dramatic developmental changes occurring during the maturation of flower buds are shown.

28. The University's Botanic Gardens have provided opportunities for staff in Biological Sciences to conduct research. Richard Gornall, Director of the Harold Martin Botanic Garden, is shown removing stamens from a tobacco plant for anther culture work.

29. The Botanic Garden includes collections of plants that have been gathered worldwide. Richard Gornall brought back a Snake Palm (Amorphophallus Prainii) from Indonesia in 1997. As the picture illustrates, it is not among the most fragrant of plants!

30. Researchers in the Department of Biology have used DNA evidence from Exmoor ponies to establish their pre-historic origins.

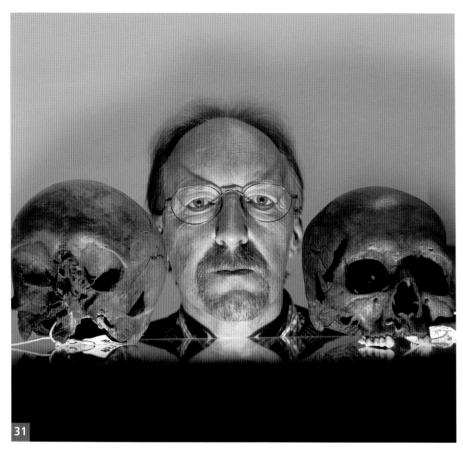

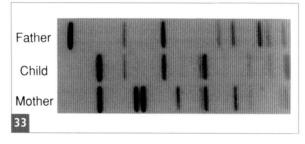

31. Members of the Archaeology Department have engaged in digs in many parts of the City and the County. In 2004 Leicester's archaeologists found the earliest human remains ever to be uncovered in the County. Dr Patrick Clay, Joint Director of the University of Leicester Archaeology Service is pictured with the excavated remains.

32. Leicester has developed an international reputation for research in geographical information science following the establishment of the Midlands Regional Research Laboratory in the Department of Geography from the early 1990s. This has provided staff and students with a valuable resource for research and teaching, enabling them to analyse large data sets using the latest technology.

33. Leicester is world renowned in the field of genetics as a result of the discovery of DNA fingerprinting by Professor Sir Alec Jeffreys in the mid-1980s. An example of the family relationship in DNA fingerprinting is illustrated.

34. The School of Archaeology and Ancient History, together with the University of Leicester Archaeological Service, were commissioned to excavate the City Centre in Leicester prior to the Highcross Shopping Centre being built. This provided a major opportunity for archaeological research and resulted in many Roman finds being discovered, such as a bath house, the town wall and a number of objects including a medieval curse tablet. The site was visited by Bob Burgess and Jo Wood who met David Mattingley and his team.

Some Examples of Medical Research

35. Team-based research requires continued sponsorship of human and physical resources. The team of researchers being visited by one of their sponsors, Dr Frank May, Chairman of Medisearch, were working on tuberculosis in the Department of Infection, Immunity and Inflammation. They include: Dr Rebecca Smith, Professor Mike Barer, Professor Peter Andrew and Dr Bernard Burke.

36. Professor Raymond Playford was one of the doctors who developed a breath test as a new ulcer diagnosis method.

37. Dr Aras Kadioglu, Lecturer in Respiratory Infection, has recently published his work on 'The role of Streptococcus pneumoniae virulence factors in host respiratory colonisation and disease' in *Nature Reviews Microbiology* [(2008), vol.6, no:4, 288-301]. Here the slides show upper respiratory tract colonisation by Streptococcus pneumoniae where the infection progresses from 30 minutes to 14 days after infection.

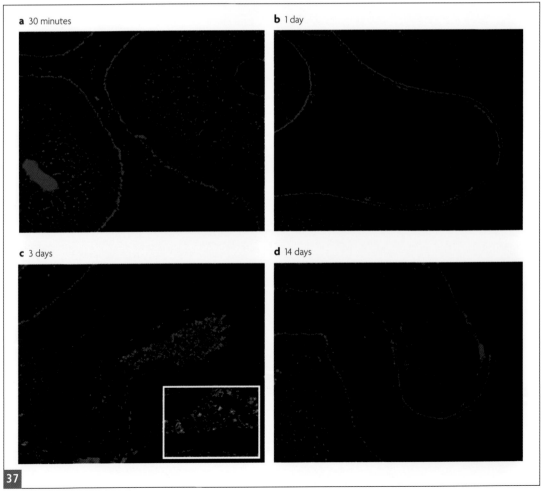

a 30 minutes

b 1 day

c 3 days

d 14 days

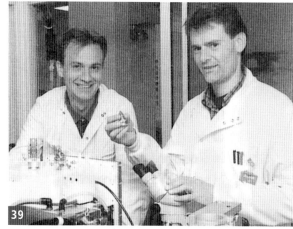

38. Research into the common cold is ongoing across the world, including at Leicester. Dr Mike McKean, a Research Fellow with the University's Department of Child Health at the Leicester Royal Infirmary in 1997, was investigating the effects on people with breathing difficulties. During this research he infected volunteers with the virus and carried out a number of tests to assess the effects of contracting the virus.

41. In 1997 a unique scheme, Hospital at Home (HAH), was trialled to provide active treatment within a patient's home for a limited period, thus enabling them to be released from hospital early. Here, Research Fellow Alison Wynn interviews Irene Shuppe, the first patient in the Hospital at Home Scheme.

39. Research is also conducted in the University on superbugs. Professor Bob Liddington and Dr Tony Maxwell from the Department of Biochemistry discovered that the structure of part of an enzyme from bacteria was able to be targeted by particular kinds of antibiotics to fight Salmonella. This work was also made available for use in industry through the University Centre for Enterprise (LUCENT).

40. Professor Liddington and Dr Carlo Petosa, were involved in collaborative research with Harvard Medical School and the National Institute of Health in Maryland, USA, into the use of biological warfare in fighting disease. The research at Leicester involved the study of proteins which make up the lethal anthrax toxin. These can be used to carry health proteins into the cells of patients who lack them or who carry abnormal forms, in particular for Muscular Dystrophy patients.

Some Research Highlights

42. Lecturer in the Department of Othopaedic Surgery, John Hardy, showing off his claim to fame; the revolutionary new shin pads designed, in collaboration with the Engineering Department, for soccer superstar Paul Gascoigne in 1995!

43. In 1993 the University of Leicester's Department of Radiology took delivery of a new Magnetic Resonance Imager (MRI). This facility has since enabled researchers to undertake clinical service work and medical education alongside their research.

44. At the heart of research activity is the presentation of research findings in seminars and workshops. In the School of Historical Studies Professor Rob Colls has developed the New History Lab that brings together postgraduate research students, who are setting out on their research careers, alongside staff members and academic visitors. It is an opportunity to bring new initiatives and new developments to the attention of other researchers in the School and in the University.

45. Professor Alison Yarrington, previously Head of the Department of History of Art looking through some of the University's wealth of material in this subject area.

46. A selection of books by University academic staff in the University Bookshop.

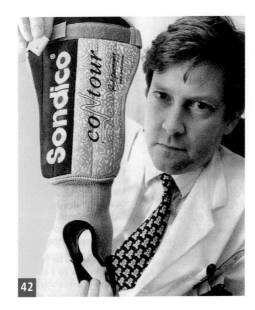

5. People

Universities include many different groups of people: staff; students; and members of the local community, some of whom serve on University committees and others who support a range of University events. Perhaps not surprisingly, when one thinks about staff in a university, the automatic reaction is to think of academics. However, this is far from the reality of life in the contemporary university. Leicester employs more support staff in administrative, clerical, manual, and technical roles than it does academics and is the third largest employer in the City. In 2008, the University employed approximately 3,500 staff who were drawn predominantly from Leicester and Leicestershire. At the same time, the total student population was approximately 21,500. In this Chapter, we have reflected these different groups of people by drawing on photographs of staff and students, some of whom will be very well known and others far less so.

It is important that all staff work together as a cohesive team, whether it involves planning for special events or engaging in day-to-day activities. Among regular events in the University calendar are Open Days for prospective undergraduates and their parents. At first glance these events may seem to rely on departmental activity and academic staff. However, to deliver an Open Day that successfully contextualises the work of departments it is important to demonstrate that the University can offer excellent facilities and a first-class student experience. Successful events therefore rely on a wide range of University staff who work together to ensure that every visit to the University is a high quality

experience. The success of an Open Day might, therefore, rest upon whether a car parking space can be found through the assistance of a porter or a member of the security staff. Alternatively, the provision of friendly service by waitresses in the Café Piazza after a long journey to Leicester might make the difference between accepting or rejecting a Leicester offer. In turn, a walk around the residences with student ambassadors might also be influential; at this point in the visit half a day may have elapsed without an encounter with the department or any of its academics.

For many students, choosing the University of Leicester may be the result of knowing about a particular researcher who teaches on the undergraduate programme or who has established a specific course or written a particular book or article that captures the imagination. As we have seen in previous Chapters, in Leicester, teaching and research are linked together with the result that the people who teach undergraduates also engage in research.

Across its fifty year history, Leicester has been fortunate in having many academics who are world renowned in their discipline. For example, in English, Professor Philip Collins was a distinguished Dickens scholar. Similarly, in Social and Economic History, Professor Jim Dyos was the leading contributor to the study of urban history in the UK and organized numerous conferences and meetings as well as establishing Leicester's highly successful Centre for Urban History. In the field of Mass Communications, Professor James

Halloran was responsible not only for initiating his Leicester Centre but also defining the discipline worldwide. For many years he was the President of the International Association of Mass Communications Research.

In Medicine, John Swales, the founding Professor, not only made contributions to research but also to local healthcare provision by training a cadre of staff who have likewise made a significant contribution to medicine. In 2008, Professors Nilesh Samani and Bryan Williams from Cardiovascular Sciences are seen not only on the international conference platform and as members of major committees at the Wellcome Trust and the Medical Research Council but also on the wards of either the Glenfield Hospital or the Royal Infirmary.

Some staff in the University are remembered not only for the posts that they occupied but also for the subsequent development of their careers. The first Dean of the Leicester Medical School, for example, remained in the University for just three years and left before the first intake of students in 1975 moving to become Vice-Chancellor and Principal of the University of Stirling. Another well-known member of staff who served the University for thirty years was Gerald Bernbaum. He began his career as a lecturer in the School of Education which he led to prominence in the UK in the 1980s. Subsequently he became one of the Pro-Vice-Chancellors and uniquely Executive Pro-Vice-Chancellor and Registrar at Leicester before moving on to take up the post of Vice-Chancellor and Chief Executive of South Bank University in 1993.

Similarly, students sometimes become well known either in their year group, department or when they have moved on from Leicester. Aaron Porter, who graduated from Leicester with a degree in English, took on the role of Academic Affairs Officer (President) of the Students' Union Executive and then moved to London to work as the Vice-President of the National Union of Students. There is no typical Leicester student; students may study for undergraduate or postgraduate degrees or both, and they can study on campus or by distance learning on a part-time or a full-time basis. Originally all students were campus-based but in the 1990s Leicester initiated distance learning programmes which in 2008 constituted 37% of the student body. Staff members may also study with the University, usually on a part-time basis, for degrees such as the BA in Humanities that has proved very popular following on from courses offered through adult education (now the Institute of Lifelong Learning). Meanwhile, others study for higher degrees with Masters' programmes proving very popular.

The Students' Union staff can also become equally well known to generations of students. For example, Phil Kirk, the General Manager, worked in the University of Leicester Students' Union for thirty two years until 2008. The Union also employs other groups of staff including cleaners, cashiers, bar and retail staff. A visit to the Union Shop will find permanent staff working alongside some students who are engaged in part-time employment to help fund their University career. Work experience is one of the many ways in which students become involved in the wider community alongside other initiatives including volunteering, membership of sports clubs, participation in clubs and societies, all of which provide opportunities to meet new friends drawn from areas of the University other than those in which they study.

Finally, the University draws on a vast range of individuals to fill many voluntary positions on its Court and Council. The University Court includes representatives of the City and County Councils, Members of Parliament and the European Parliament together with representatives of religious bodies and other organisations. The Council is the University's governing body, and includes lay members chosen for their expertise in areas such as law, finance, business and other related occupations. They bring a valuable external view to the University. It is also the University's good fortune to have strong support from some of its Honorary Graduates, the best known of whom nationally and internationally are Richard and David Attenborough whose father was the second Principal of University College Leicester. They are great patrons of the University, the City and County alongside numerous others, including some who will be far less well-known or instantly recognisable. Nevertheless, many of these supporters regularly appear in University photographs.

Unsung Heroes

1. There are few more important people to a University than its cleaners. In 1965 *Ripple* reported 'Situation Acute – Cleaners' Crisis' as a staff shortage had the potential to create considerable disruption within the Halls of Residence. Warden, Richard Bishop, said the situation 'is as acute as I have ever known it' although the Vice-Chancellor (Sir Fraser Noble) commented that he 'was not aware of any immediate crisis [and] each hall had kept going by using differing techniques, in the face of extremely adverse economic circumstances'. This highlights the importance of support staff, whose contributions to the effective running of the University, are essential and must not be overlooked.

2. Another group of individuals vital to the success of the University were the staff within the Health Centre which opened in October 1967 and, as reported in *Ripple* on 11 January 1968, was immediately 'an unqualified success'.

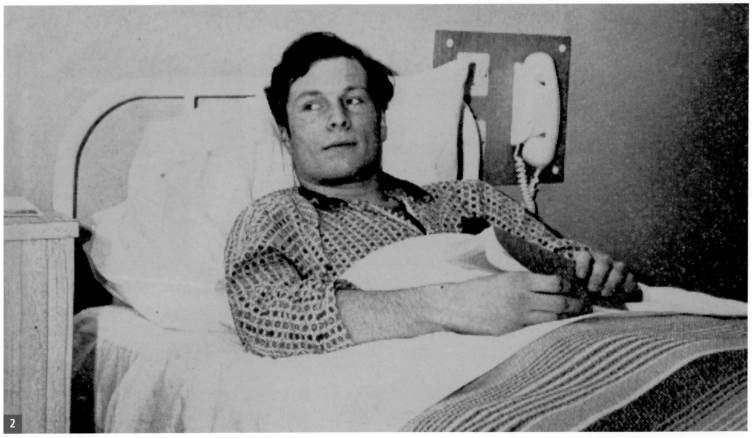

3-4. If you venture into the Student Union Shop at around 1pm you will often find the current Vice-Chancellor buying his lunch! This important facility has been serving the University community since the 1960s. As *Ripple* reported on 14 June 1973, its primary function was to provide stationery but it also diversified into selling sweets, tobacco, sportswear, University-branded goods and so on. In this respect it has changed little, although in 1973 it provided an additional function, as *Ripple* commented: 'it benefits the students in more ways than one – for Mrs Ward and co. act as unofficial Marjorie Proops for students in distress. Because homesick young first-years can identify them with their own mothers, the lost and bewildered eighteen-year-old away from home for the first time can go to this friendly gaggle for understanding and sympathy.'

5. In May 1989 the staff newsletter *Bulletin* reported that if you ever wanted to know anything about the University, Terry Garfield in the Geography Department was the person to contact. Terry was Chief Technician and was a mine of information as he had worked in the University for over 40 years. Not only Terry, but also members of his family worked for the University. His wife Sylvia was Chief Clerk in English and his brother Ken worked in the Central Photographic Unit. They undoubtedly saw many changes over the years, not least in the area of technology. During an interview with the *Bulletin*, Terry commented "I am very proud of the University and the Department. I hope that I have made some contribution to the high standards that we set." On his retirement in 1992 Terry was awarded an Honorary Degree in recognition of his 46 years with the University during which time he had been a founder member of the Departmental Staff Common Room Association in which he continues to play an active role by arranging a full and varied programme of social events.

Long Service

6. In some departments staff have clocked-up a huge record of service, having joined the University when they left school. In 1993, the Geography Department and the Central Photographic Unit celebrated the combined centenary of service achieved by four members of their staff who joined the University in 1968. A surprise party was organised by friends and colleagues for Ruth Rowell and Brian Kernan (Geography) and Ian Paterson and Henryk Kowalski (CPU).

7. Shortly after his arrival at the University, the current Vice-Chancellor became increasingly aware of the large numbers of staff who had long service with the University. He felt it was important to mark this achievement by hosting an annual lunch for staff who had completed 25, 30, 35 and even 40 years' service. This has become a regular feature in the University calendar; for example, in July 2001 a group of 23 staff celebrated 25 years' service. They were drawn from all areas of the University but it gave an opportunity for those who had worked together to meet up in a social setting including Margaret Smith (Manager of College Hall) and Johnathan Young (Warden of College Hall).

Retirements

8. When the Students' Union became independent of the University, there was an opportunity for staff to become employees of the Union. Frank Burrows was the only porter who made this transition and contributed nine years' service, retiring in January 1977.

9. Another important team is the staff who work in the University's Gardens, both on University Road and in Oadby. The Gardens are the responsibility of the Estates Department, so when Sid Cadle, Head Gardener and Head Groundsman, retired from the University it was Richard Float, then Bursar with responsibility for Estates, who toasted Sid and his wife at a party to celebrate Sid's retirement in June 1990.

10. The University would also find it impossible to function without its extensive maintenance staff of carpenters, plumbers, electricians, painters and so on. Graham Smith, carpenter/joiner, pictured with his wife Christine, Mick Williams (Security), Dougie Vukelic (Porter in the Charles Wilson Building) and Alan Summers (Maintenance) at Graham's retirement reception in 1997.

11. John Burns worked within the University for nearly twenty three years as a painter and decorator, but also served as Unison Branch Chairman for 13 years. He was delighted to be presented with a cheque and gift by Simon Britton (then Director of Estates) at a celebratory event on Friday 6 August 2004 when colleagues from around the University gathered to wish him well on his retirement.

12. Many members of the University, including those working for Corporate Services, are involved in other areas of activity alongside their day jobs. Jim Kelly, a plumber in the Estates Department, was well-known for his involvement in establishing the University Branch of the National Union of Public Employees (NUPE which has now become UNISON). Colleagues and friends gathered to wish him a long and happy retirement after twenty three years' service to the University.

Some Personal Stories

13

14

13. The University encourages students with disabilities to apply to study at Leicester. For example, Marjorie Needham gained her first degree in Sociology in 1994. Many students have been highly successful with the support of the AccessAbility Centre that provides assistance for those with a range of learning difficulties and disabilities.

14. It is not only young people straight from school or college who take degrees at Leicester. Many mature students and members of staff also take the opportunity to benefit from their learning environment and develop new skills in a range of different subject areas. Janet Graham, Head of Admissions and Student Recruitment (pictured), who received an MA in Historical Studies in 1997 said: "Why did I do it? It was for interest and to prove to myself that I could! I thoroughly enjoyed the MA, but I don't think I will be doing any more part-time study just yet." Joining her that year in graduation celebrations at the De Montfort Hall, the following members of staff also received their degrees: Ivan Waddington, Director of the Centre for Research into Sport and Society, received a PhD in Sociology; Natalia Stephens, who had worked in the Estates and Services Department, received a BA in Humanities.

15-16. Leicester has also seen many members of the same family studying for its degrees, sometimes at the same time. Mutual congratulations were the order of the day for mother and daughter Sue and Jennie Mailley as they received their degree certificates in July 1997 – Sue receiving an MA in Professional Studies in Education and Jennie a BSc in Medical Biochemistry (15). At the degree celebrations in July 2000, the then Dean of the Medical School, Ian Lauder, was very proud to present his son, Chris, with the degree of MBChB (16).

17. Raman Verna celebrates gaining his MB PhD, the first double doctorate awarded by the University of Leicester in 2004.

18-19. Winning awards is a feature of University life. In the early 1990s Catering staff won the Heart Beat catering award for healthy eating. Additionally, the University's Central Catering Services won its second Food Safety Award against a background of increasingly demanding legislation. Feeding 6,000 people a day, with a turnover of £1.7 million in 12 outlets in 1996 was a considerable challenge. As Malcolm Brown, Catering Services Director, commented in *Bulletin*: "The inspector was with us for eight or nine hours, examining fridges, floors and work surfaces. Staff were interviewed to test their knowledge and they passed with flying colours." In 2008, catering staff fed around 7,000 people per day, turning over in excess of £2.3 million in 14 outlets.

20. Professor of Ancient History in the School of Archaeology and Ancient History, Lin Foxhall, was awarded an MBE (Hon) for her involvement with a project funded at £3 million by the Millennium Commission (National Lottery) called 'Ringing in the Millennium'. This entailed the restoration and augmentation of church bells nationwide to celebrate the millennium – most of which rang in the New Year on 1 January 2000. The Royal Mail also issued a stamp commemorating the successful project in marking the new Millennium.

21. The University's video production unit, AVS Video, has been showered with awards over recent years. Here, the team is shown receiving the Learning on Screen Premier Award, the top award for non-broadcast entries, for their production commissioned by Oadby, Wigston and South Wigston Domestic Violence Forum 'Understanding Domestic Abuse'. The awards are the UK education equivalent of the Oscars and are designed to promote the 'use of innovative learning design and production creativity'. Other accolades have included Best Editing category, Training Award for a video about the Leicester Royal Infirmary Prematurity Prevention Service and in 2006 the unit won two top awards at the HeSCA (Health and Science Communications Association) 2006 Media Festival for their DVD 'Recognising Risk and Improving Patient Safety' commissioned by Dr Liz Anderson in the Department of Medical and Social Care Education.

Some Well-Known Names and Faces in the University

22. The then Executive Pro-Vice-Chancellor and Registrar Professor Gerry Bernbaum (left), receives the gift of a rug from Dr Ken Edwards (right) on leaving the University to become Vice-Chancellor of London's South Bank University in 1993. He was well-known not only for his formal roles but also as a cricket supremo who regularly played for the staff team.

24-25. The Attenborough family has a long association with the University since Frederick Attenborough was Principal of University College. His sons, Richard and David have been regular visitors over the years. On Wednesday 23 April 1997, as part of the University's Jubilee year, Sir David Attenborough returned to the University to formally open the Attenborough Arboretum, before delivering a public lecture entitled Revealing the Private Life of Plants.

23. Professor Jack Spence was a major figure in Leicester's Politics Department who subsequently became a Pro-Vice-Chancellor before his appointment as Director of Chatham House in London. He received an Honorary Degree from the University in 2001.

26-27. Staff within the University regularly engage in student recruitment activity in the UK and overseas. The Director of Press and Publications, Ather Mirza, visited Kenya in 1998, some 26 years since he had lived there as a child. During his visit he also met a number of Leicester graduates who were taking key roles in Kenyan society as a result of having studied for a UK degree.

28. Professor Ken Pounds transformed the University's Physics Department through his development of X-ray astronomy and contributions to the Space Research Centre and the National Space Centre. In the 1990s he was seconded as Chief Executive of PPARC (the Particle Physics and Astronomy Research Council) whose Chairman was Sir Peter Williams, who subsequently became the University's Chancellor in 2005.

29. Professor John Holloway joined the Chemistry Department in the 1960s and played a major role in the development of the subject and the University by serving as Head of Department, Dean of the Faculty of Science and Pro-Vice-Chancellor with responsibility for Learning and Teaching.

30. Professor Sarah Spurgeon has been an important role model for women students wishing to study Engineering. In a *Times Higher Education Supplement* article in 2007, Sarah, Head of Leicester's Department of Engineering at the time, discussed the importance of women taking a larger role within wider management. She believes it is only then that strategies can move forward, commenting 'Out of 32 staff, we have just three female academics – and we are much better than most engineering departments. I think for us to see a culture change, women who reach senior positions need to draw on their own skills rather than trying to behave like men'.

31. Staff are involved in many activities throughout the University, aside from their day-to-day jobs. These include participating in staff/student sports teams, undertaking courses, learning new languages, singing in the choir or playing in the orchestra or taking advantage of relaxation classes run by the Welfare Service. Margaret Rose, who has worked at the University for over 20 years, enjoys her weekly Latin American dance course at The Richard Attenborough Centre. "It's great fun and good exercise," she says.

32. Professor Sir Alec Jeffreys is arguably the most famous member of Leicester's staff, having discovered DNA fingerprinting in 1984. He is credited with a range of major discoveries and received numerous awards including becoming a Fellow of the Royal Society in his thirties and being knighted in his forties. He still works in the laboratory where he has continued to develop the field of medical genetics, winning the prestigious Louis Jeantet prize in 2004.

Student Activities

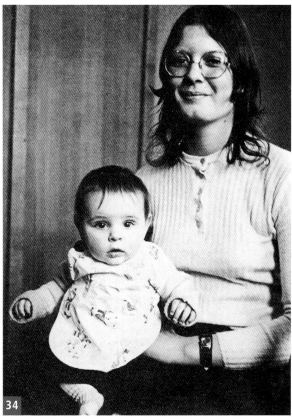

33. Among the bands, employers, health workers and other visitors to the Students' Union have been MPs invited to talk on a range of topics. In November 1977 the Union hosted the Leader of the Liberal Party, David Steel MP, who was a keynote speaker at the University Liberal Students' Conference in Leicester at which he attacked the National Front saying "We should not forget that although it professes to put forward a legitimate political programme, the basic motivating force behind that programme is based on naked facism and intolerance." This speech was regarded as highly significant as at that time a sixth of the City's 300,000 population were from a variety of ethnic backgrounds.

34. One might imagine that the demands by parents for crèches to be provided at their place of work and study are relatively new. However, in the early 1970s campus mothers were demanding crèche facilities for their children. A survey for the University's Women's Liberation Group reported in *Ripple* on 1 March 1973 indicated that a number of staff and students would welcome the crèche provision. Whilst the Group supported the view that "children are more important than studies" they did not feel that childcare needs should prevent students (usually women) from being involved in higher education. The Students' Union supported this position by providing half of the funding to convert a suitable room in their building for a crèche. Currently, the University has an arrangement for childcare provision through childcare vouchers.

35. In 1972, students even engaged in croquet on the lawns at Stamford Hall!

36-39. While Leicester has a wealth of academic and pastoral activities to offer potential students, we thought it would be remiss not to include these photographs which clearly play to the stereotype of students drinking in a variety of bars – a theme that has been used over the years in the undergraduate prospectus!

40

41

45

43

42

44

40. Wayne Gilby and Richard Muscle found the new sand filled all-weather pitch was not as weather-proof as they had hoped when snow and ice stopped play in 1998!

41-45. Leicester has had many sporting talents amongst its student body and its rugby, football, hockey and cricket teams, amongst others, regularly compete against other universities. The Inter-Hall matches and annual Varsity competitions against De Montfort University are fiercely contested. Students also have the opportunity to take part in many non-traditional sporting activities whilst at Leicester including dance, judo, rowing, climbing and lacrosse.

Key Supporters and Honorary Graduates

46-47. Leicester has a number of people to whom it is indebted for their support and promotion of the University. A complete list would be very long but it would inevitably include Freda Hussein, Helen Scott, Frank and Katherine May (46) and Jean Humphreys (47). Following a long connection with the University through her husband Arthur, who was Founding Professor of English, Jean has donated a number of works of art to the University including the University Clock outside the Charles Wilson Building and the Noon Mark outside the Attenborough Seminar Block. Frank and Katherine May have also supported the University, especially the Medical School, and it was for this reason that the Lecture Theatre in the Henry Wellcome Building was named after them in 2005. In 2007 local builder and businessman David Wilson (48) also became a major benefactor of the University through his support for the new University Library. The building was named after him and officially opened by Her Majesty the Queen and the Duke of Edinburgh on Thursday 4 December 2008.

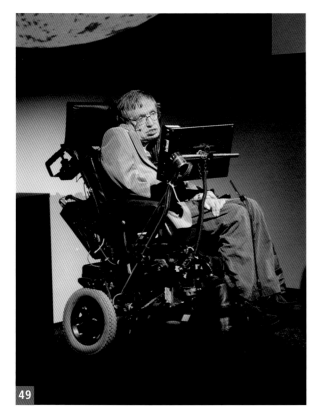

49-53. Leicester has been fortunate over the years as many well-known, national, celebrities have accepted an Honorary Degree. These include Frank Whittle (1960 – inventor of the jet engine), Benjamin Britten (1965 – composer), Yehudi Menuhin (1965 – violinist), Iris Murdoch (1982 – novelist), Stephen Hawking (1982 – scientist)(49), Joan Hickson (1988 – actress)(53), Betty Boothroyd (1993 – politician)(52), Lord Richard and Sir David Attenborough (1970 and Distinguished Honorary Fellowships in 2006 – film and TV producers)(50), and Karl Jenkins (2007 – composer)(51).

54-58. Leicester has also been able to honour those more well-known within their local community for their good work within the City and County. These include Sue Townsend (1991 and Distinguished Honorary Fellowship 2008 – novelist, famous for the *Adrian Mole* books), Jean Humphreys (2001 and Distinguished Honorary Fellowship 2008– great supporter and benefactor of the University)(54), Elvy Morton (2001 – organiser of the Leicester Caribbean Carnival for 16 years)(57), Sir Tim and the Hon Lady Ann Brooks (2002 and 2003 – former Lord Lieutenant and Honorary Canon of Leicester Cathedral respectively), the Rt Revd Tim Stevens (2003 – Bishop of Leicester)(56), the Very Revd Derek Hole (2005 – Emeritus Provost of Leicester Cathedral), Keith Julian (2007 – former Registrar of the University)(58) and Linda Jones (2007 – former Chief Probation Officer of Leicestershire and National Offender Manager)(55).

59. Honorary Graduates, Baroness Amos and Laurie Taylor, and senior officers of the University of Leicester celebrating the end of the summer degree congregation with an ice cream (purchased from the ice-cream van parked outside the De Montfort Hall) on 14 July 2006!

6. Communities

Members of the University belong to many different communities within Leicester, Leicestershire, Rutland and the East Midlands region. It is the relationship between the University and the surrounding areas on which this Chapter focuses although any university also relates to a wide range of communities nationally and internationally.

When people talk about 'the University community', they usually mean relationships between staff and students. However, this is an extremely narrow perspective as in 2007/08 the University consisted of over 19,000 students, almost 3,500 staff as well as numerous visitors who came onto the campus during the year. Students from both Universities within the City constitute 10% of Leicester's population. In addition, academics, administrators, gardeners, cleaners, secretarial staff, technicians, porters and many others all form a range of different communities within the institution and beyond it. The University is the size of a small town with all the issues, problems and successes that accompany this kind of population but it also contributes considerably to the local economy estimated at approximately £0.5 billion to the region.

Although well-known for being a diverse and multi-cultural city, Leicester is much more than that. It is vibrant, busy and green – a City with a keen interest in the arts that has for some time been an environmental city. In 1990 it was awarded the status of Britain's first Environmental City and its EcoHouse re-opened in 2000. The University contributes widely to the City, the County and the region. In particular, it supports a wide range of organisations including those concerned with economic development and regeneration, health and charitable work. University staff also contribute to a variety of organisations such as local churches, hospitals, schools, museums and criminal justice agencies.

The University provides a number of services through its academic departments. Most well known is the contribution the Department of Physics and Astronomy has made to the foundation and development of the National Space Centre in Leicester. Consultancy services are offered in almost every subject area that the University provides, spin-out companies have been established in many areas such as security and risk management and healthcare provision. The University's independent archaeological unit has also been involved in several major excavations in the City and County, in particular a Bronze Age cemetery and Anglo-Saxon settlement near Melton Mowbray. It was responsible for excavating all the major sites around Leicester's inner ring road in preparation for the development of the extended Shires and Highcross Shopping area that opened in 2008.

Another well-known aspect of the University's contribution to the local population is through its Medical School. Many local GPs were trained in the University and leading consultants who work both for the University and local hospitals regularly treat patients. Other subject areas provide professional training that takes place locally in schools and social work settings. Many Leicester-trained teachers and social workers decide to take up employment in the City and County as well as elsewhere following graduation.

Students are also enthusiastic about giving something back to the community through a number of clubs and societies that are organised within the Students' Union. For example, CONTACT (the student volunteering society), RAG (the student charities association), and the Teddy Bears Hospital (a society where medical students work with children to allay their fears about going into hospital). The University's music societies include orchestral and choral groups that have staged concerts and other productions over many years that are open to all. Other cultural activities involving both the local and University communities include events such as productions by Leicester University Theatre; the Annual Sculpture Show in the Harold Martin Botanic Garden; the development of a loan and donation scheme for local artists to display their work within the University; and the activities run by the Richard Attenborough Centre.

The University engages in many community activities through working with MPs and MEPs, involvement in the City's regeneration scheme, developing Leicester's sporting reputation, and building relationships with major businesses and organisations such as the Leicester Chamber of Commerce and the Leicester Asian Business Association. It also recognises the contribution that individuals make to society locally, nationally and internationally by including many people from the locality in its award of Honorary Degrees and Distinguished Honorary Fellowships. Some aspects of the University's involvement in the community is portrayed in the pictures that follow.

Enhancing the Environment

1. The University's Harold Martin Botanic Garden is named after the University's first Registrar and Secretary. It is open to members of the public throughout the year; providing a haven of tranquillity within the bustling Oadby student village. The Curator, Dr Richard Gornall, provides an educational programme for schools that includes wildlife and environmental issues. In 1999 Mitchell Greasley of Syston was delighted to be awarded a token of appreciation for being the 10,000th schoolchild through the gates of the Garden.

2. Staff at the University also take great pride in the appearance of their workplace. John Benyon and his team in the Scarman Centre (now the Department of Criminology) regularly had a display of hanging baskets and tubs. In 1994 judges from the Leicester in Bloom competition visited and gave them top marks for the second year running in the Best Institution section. When he became Director of Lifelong Learning, John Benyon continued the tradition of providing hanging baskets outside the Institute.

3. The University has long held a desire to ensure that its surroundings are attractive to its staff, students and members of the wider community and has regularly acquired works of art to enhance the environment. Amongst many others, a sculpture by Robert Adams entitled *Triangulated Structure Number 1* is located on the central campus.

4. A nail sculpture *Thorn Crucifix* by David Partridge, presented to the University by Convocation, hangs in the entrance to the Rattray Lecture Theatre.

5. The University has widened its art collection often through donations and loans by local artists. Joyce Markie, an artist based in Market Harborough, is renowned for her work on space and has presented pictures to the University over many years. She is shown next to her work, inspired by images from the Hubble Space Telescope, in the Department of Physics and Astronomy with (l-r) Dr Brin Cooke, Professor Iain Davidson, former High Sheriff Mr Robin Murray-Phillipson and Mrs Nina Murray-Phillipson. Another of Joyce's works, *Cats Eye Nebula*, which she donated in 2005, is located in the Henry Wellcome Building.

6. *Bluebells* by Charles Bezzina, based in Northamptonshire, was donated to the University by the artist. The picture was used on the cover of the Degree Ceremony Brochure in the summer of 2007.

Community Activities

7. The Richard Attenborough Centre (RAC) was established to provide a resource for disabled and able-bodied members of the local community wishing to become more involved in the arts. Among its regular classes are subjects as diverse as singing, sculpture, life drawing and salsa dancing.

8-9. The RAC provides a delightful venue for concerts and exhibitions. Celebrating its first summer in 1997 the Centre put on a lively display of art, dance, theatrical and musical activities during Arts Week which required participants to be skilled in a wide range of areas, not least furniture removal!

10. In 2005 the Botanic Garden was fortunate to be chosen as the venue for the Royal British Society of Sculptors Centenary event, which attracted a wide range of artists including Mary Anstee-Parry (Fishweave). The show draws a large audience into the Garden over the summer period each year and is very popular with the local community.

11. Jay Battle *Slated Divide* also displayed work at the sculpture show in 2005.

12. *Souls* is a major sculpture on the Fielding Johnson lawn on the central campus, shown here with the sculptor, Helaine Blumenfeld, who led the University's Annual Sculpture Show for six years (2002-2007).

Hosting Events for the Public

13. The University plays host to a variety of organisations including radio and television programmes. On 22 and 23 April 1987 the BBC took over the Fraser Noble Hall for the television programme *Mastermind*.

14. Ten years' later, on 10 September 1997, *Gardeners' Question Time* came to Gilbert Murray Hall. In the academic year 2002, the University celebrated the 80th Anniversary of the establishment of University College and as part of a series of wide-ranging activities the programme visited again.

15. *Any Questions?* was broadcast from the University for a second time on 22 November 2002.

Charity Events

16. Many Leicester students are involved in voluntary work whilst at University especially through CONTACT, the student volunteering organisation. After graduation some go on to undertake voluntary work in the community before setting out on a career. For some this also influences their choice of future career, such as those who go on to become teachers. Catherine Gray, a Biological Sciences graduate in 2000, for example, decided to take part in a Raleigh International expedition to Chile where she is shown with a class of children.

17. RAG week is well known to generations of students. Indeed, one of the inevitable enjoyments of being a student is getting involved in charitable events such as RAG and Red Nose Day. In particular, the events are even more fun if one can get a Pro-Vice-Chancellor, such as Professor Ian Postlethwaite, to take part! Although RAG eventually changed its name to Leicester University Charitable Appeal (LUCA), its aim to raise funds for local and national charities has remained as strong as ever. Over the years many activities have been enjoyed by students and staff for the benefit of others.

Poor communication between individuals in the Rag '76 organisation is blamed, by members of Beaumont Hall Bar Committee for angry scenes which occurred during the Hall's Rag Disco between Rag Publicity Officer, Bob Fogg and Beaumont Hall's Social Secretary, John Weedon.

RIPPLE interviewed Bar Manager, John Sullivan, who gave the Beaumont Hall side of the story. He claims that Rag promised to supply ten people to help clear up after the Disco. The extra help failed to appear and so John Weedon asked Beaumont's Rag Rep. Steve Samaroff, and Rag Publicity Officer to stay and help, Bob Fogg claimed he was too tired and refused to stay at which point John Weedon became angry and had to be physically restrained from attacking Bob Fogg by Neil Fowler (Beaumont Hall Vice President). Bob Fogg left at this stage though he later returned.

Rag-deputy Chairman, Nick Gould was

"RAG IN TATTERS" CHARGE AFTER BEAUMONT FIASCO
REPORT BY PAUL NETTLETON

contacted in Digby and eventually brought ten people from Digby and STamford to help. Rag paid these people varying amounts of cash between 50p and £1.

Further problems occurred when, on Thursday, Jon Wright, John Sullivan and John Weedon visited the Rag Office to discuss the situation and to collect five complimentary tickets promised earlier by Rag Entertainments Officer, Phil Johnson, in return for Beaumont's co-operation with Rag. Nick Gould attempted to overrule Phil Johnson and offered only two tickets.

After further discussion he relented, and also agreed to the payment

of 50p each to members of Beaumont Hall bar staff - a number of whom had spent the day setting up bars and rearranging furniture for the evening.

Beaumont Bar Committee issued the following statement as a general criticism of the Rag '76 organisation and of their conduct in the organisation of the Beaumont Rag Disco:

"This appalling lack of organisation and co-ordination has in my mind been symptomatic of the whole of Rag this year; posters have been badly produced, uninformative and insufficient for effective publicity. Even within the committee communication

seems to have been pratically non-existent, (this is typified by the way in which "Big Will" was dealt with. If you see him let him tell you of the organisation?)"

RAG-deputy Chairman refused to comment when approached by RIPPLE, indicating that he would prefer to discuss the matter further before making a public statement.

Only 50% of Clare Hall's profits from its Rag Disco went to Rag as a result of what Jill Allen, Clare Hall President, described as the 'failure of Rag to provide adequate publicity and to offer help for the evening.'

21

20

UNIVERSITY OF LEICESTER

RAG & GIVING MAG 2005

19

18. Things did not always turn out as students' expected and in 1976 RAG was something of a dog's dinner…
(*Ripple*, May 4 1976).

19. RAG Mags are synonymous with students' 'raising and giving' activities. Looked at from the 21st Century, RAG Mags from the 50s and 60s would be seen as politically incorrect and whilst they still contain items such as 'The Five Stages of Drunkenness' gone are the risqué jokes and other material that could be considered offensive.

20. Abseiling down the Attenborough Tower for charity.

21. Former Cabinet Minister, Reg Prentice, was not amused when he was kidnapped by RAG as he spoke at a Union lecture in February 1977. He was placed on a platform under the Market Place arch and the RAG Chairman suggested 10p for a kiss or handshake with him which attracted a large crowd. However, after getting over the initial shock, he was reported by *Ripple* to have taken the whole thing very well.

Societies

22. Another aspect of University life is the wide range of societies available to students to participate in leisure time activities. The Students' Union has over 100 clubs and societies for its members. The University Orchestra was established in 1967 but gave its inaugural concert in the Queen's Hall in October 1969. Initially it performed in local schools but soon after began to give recitals and concerts within the University and the local community and continues to perform in the Fraser Noble Hall and at St James the Greater Church, among other venues.

23. Despite studying for a demanding degree Runa Saha, a Leicester medical student in 1997, joined other medical students keen to get together for musical, cultural and social activities in forming a new symphony orchestra,

modelled on its European counterpart, the European Medical Students' Orchestra.

24. In the early 1970s many students were able to enjoy the experience of preparing the University programme 'Campus' at Radio Leicester, and this led to the establishment of LUSH FM, the University's first student radio station, in 1998.

25. Funded by the Students' Union, LUSH continues to operate alongside other student initiatives such as the Student Newspaper, *Ripple*, and Leicester University Student Television (LUST) which provide students with an opportunity to gain invaluable work experience in a media environment.

26. Many of the societies have been established for a long period of time, including Leicester University Theatre, shown here in their production of *The Little Shop of Horrors*.

27. French students also produced an annual performance, shown here in *Alequin a la foire* (Lesage).

28. Another production performed on the steps of the Fielding Johnson Building is that of *The Three Musketeers*.

Schools' Liaison

29-31. Students are the best ambassadors for the University and Leicester has made a key feature of using its own students to guide prospective students and their parents around the campus during its Open Days. These students also help promote the University by assisting with other major events such as visits to local schools.

32. The University works with many local schools to encourage young people in the City and County to consider continuing with their studies in higher education. For example, Leicestershire students had the opportunity to see how chemistry is used every day during a 'Chemistry at Work' Exhibition organised by the Royal Society of Chemistry in 1992 with the co-operation of local and national companies.

33-34. Subsequently, numerous similar events have taken place in a variety of departments including Genetics, Physics and Mathematics. Physics, in particular, runs regular Space Summer Schools for schoolchildren. This involves hands-on experience of making a rocket in the laboratory and launching it on the University's playing fields at its Oadby campus.

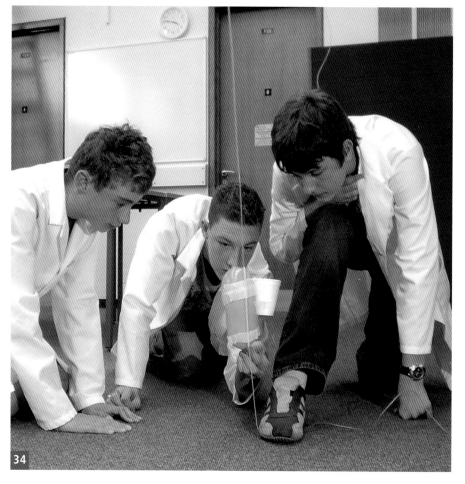

Supporting Public Services

35. Developing a University Medical School in 1973 was a turning point in health services for the citizens of Leicester, Leicestershire and Rutland. Prior to this, medical services were limited but the development of three teaching hospitals within the City has enabled many different specialties to be provided for the local community. Many eminent researchers run clinics and engage in ward rounds alongside conducting world renowned research to enhance medical provision for the wider population. Specialists provide excellent service in their fields and include Professor Nilesh Samani whose work in the field of cardiovascular science is world-class.

36. Having suffered from cardiac problems, actor Bill Maynard pledged his support to The Midlands Family Heart Study, a project spearheaded by University scientists at the Glenfield Hospital.

37. The University Chaplaincy is also involved in the work of the local hospitals. In 2005, international students visited the Leicester Royal Infirmary and presented origami cranes to cardiovascular patients; a symbol of peace, unity and well-being.

35

36

37

38-39. Another important issue affecting the community is crime. Leicester boasts a Criminology Department (formerly the Scarman Centre) and regularly assists Police, Prison and Probation Services across the country and internationally. Staff within the Scarman Centre were involved in producing many national reports on contemporary issues including *Violence in Schools* and *Gun Law* as well as books on crime and security.

40. The University works with a range of organisations including the Police. The current Vice-Chancellor, Bob Burgess, signed a Memorandum of Understanding with the Northamptonshire Police Force in 2008 enabling the newly established Forensic Science Centre to work with the Force.

Building Relationships

41-43. The Lord Mayor and Chairman of Leicestershire County Council are invited into the University on an annual basis, visiting departments of their choice in order to gain a greater understanding of the extensive teaching and research activity being undertaken. Similar visits also occur from time-to-time with other external groups including MPs and MEPs.
(41) l-r Professor Peter Williams, Head of Department of Genetics; Lord Mayor Gary Hunt; Professor Annette Cashmore, Genetics.
(42) l-r Professor Annette Cashmore, Genetics; Mr Derek Clark, MEP; Mr Roger Helmer, MEP; Mr Chris Heaton-Harris, MEP; Professor Sir Alec Jeffreys; Mr Bill Newton Dunn, MEP.
(43) l-r Dr Sue Page, Geography; Peter Winkless, Chairman of Leicestershire County Council; Professor Michael Bradshaw, Geography; and Professor Mark Thompson, Senior Pro-Vice-Chancellor.

44-45. The City of Leicester could be considered the Sports Capital of the UK as it has been the home of many distinguished sporting names including Peter Wheeler, who received an Honorary Degree from the University for his services to Rugby and Leicester Tigers. Charles Palmer (44) received an Honorary Degree for his services to Leicestershire Cricket and Gary Lineker (45) for his services to Leicester City Football Club.

46. Sue Townsend, author of the *Adrian Mole* books, pictured with Louise Jones and Christine Fyfe, views a display of her work at the David Wilson Library 2008.

47. The University Library houses materials in its Special Collections from local authors. Sue Townsend deposited an extensive collection of manuscripts, typescripts for books, plays and screenplays along with related correspondence including the handwritten manuscript for the *The Secret Diary of Adrian Mole Aged 13¾,* which originally had a different title.

48. The University Library has also acquired a range of material relating to Joe Orton, the Leicester born playwright. Among the collection is a page from Orton's scrapbook which includes newspaper cuttings about his production *Entertaining Mr Sloane*.

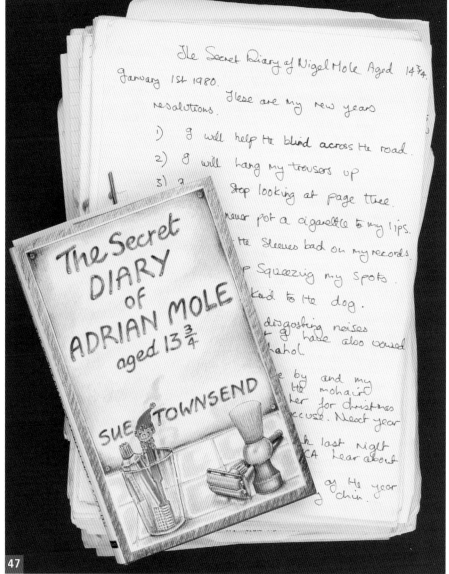

49. The University is involved with a range of different communities in multi-cultural Leicester. Many people from these communities have received Honorary Degrees from the University for their work, including Rita Patel, the founder of The Peepul Centre, an arts and social centre located in the Belgrave area of the City.

50. Englebert Humperdinck has had a home in Leicestershire throughout his career. He was given an Honorary Degree for his services to Music.

51. The actress who features in *Bend it Like Beckham* and in the well-known television programme *ER*, Parminder Nagra, was also honoured by the University with the Honorary Degree of Doctor of Letters.

Wide Ranging Links

52. The University has developed many links with communities abroad. For example, the Leicester/Pisa Research Colloquium arose out of a research agreement between the Vice-Chancellors of Leicester and Pisa in the 1990s. Annual colloquia are held alternately in Leicester and Pisa, such as the three-day 1998 colloquium on 'Metamorphosis', and collaborative research has been established in the areas of Art History, History and English.

53. Researchers at the University also have industrial and commercial connections with organisations including Jaguar, Astra Zeneca, Rolls Royce, Alliance and Leicester and De Beers. In some cases the University provides courses for these companies while in other instances the companies provide sponsorship for PhD students such as Simon Lawes in Engineering. His research was sponsored by Jaguar Cars Ltd to investigate new materials for valve-train applications which have the potential to improve engine efficiency and help to decrease harmful environmental emissions.

54. The University of Leicester Archaeological Services (ULAS) has been involved in several major excavations in the city and county. ULAS celebrated its 10th anniversary on 1 July 2005 when it held events for local children at the Jewry Wall Museum during National Archaeology Week.

55. ULAS was responsible in 2006 for conducting a major dig on both sides of the ring road in the City where the new Highcross shopping centre is located. This aerial photograph indicates work in progress on one of the sites in which ULAS was involved, next to the Free Grammar School on Highcross Street.

Controversial Issues

56. Like any other community, life does not always run smoothly and universities are not immune from experiencing periods of unrest within their communities. For example, the 1960s is often referred to as a decade of student revolution and Leicester students played their part. In 1968, students staged a four day 'sit-in' in the Fielding Johnson Building protesting against a joint staff-student working party report on Student Participation in University government.

57-58. Staff have also been involved in disputes with the institution. For example, in 1996 they were involved in a nationwide strike in protest over a national pay offer of 1.5% for academic, academic-related, clerical and technical staff. Official pickets at Leicester picketed the snowy entrances on 19 November.

59. In better weather, members of the Association of University Teachers again picketed the University entrances on 25 May 1999 as part of a nationwide protest over their claim for a 10% increase in salaries. This action was resolved but a similar issue reared its head again in 2006 when disputes took a more acute form as staff declined to mark assessed work and examination scripts.

56

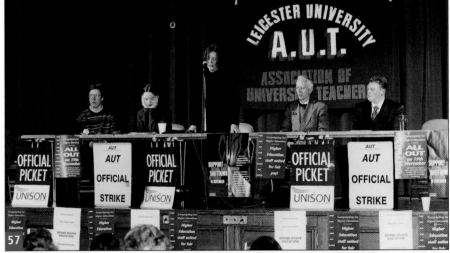
57

59

58

7. Celebrations

In the popular imagination, celebrations in universities are often associated with the award of degrees. However, this is to underplay the range of occasions, events and awards that universities are able to celebrate. Higher education has not celebrated sector-wide events until relatively recently through such competitions as 'Students' Union of the Year' (won by Leicester in 2005) and 'University of the Year' run by the *Times Higher Education* Magazine (where Leicester was shortlisted in 2005 and 2006 and won in 2008), but individual universities have many occasions to celebrate. These take numerous forms, including: the construction and opening of new buildings; exhibitions; visits by well-known local and national figures; sports competitions and achievements of staff and students.

The University's first major celebration was associated with the granting of the Royal Charter in 1957 formalising the transition from being a University College awarding degrees from the University of London to an institution able to award its own degrees. During the following academic year, the University received the first of several Royal visits when HM The Queen and HRH The Duke of Edinburgh officially opened the Percy Gee Building on 9 May 1958. As portrayed in this chapter, the University has welcomed other members of the Royal family over the years. These have included: the Duchess of Gloucester who opened the Breast Cancer Unit at Glenfield Hospital; HRH the Earl of Wessex, Prince Edward, and HRH the Countess of Wessex who visited the Richard Attenborough

Centre; and the Duke of Gloucester who opened a new facility within the Engineering Department. Finally, fifty years after her initial visit HM The Queen, accompanied by HRH The Duke of Edinburgh, opened the David Wilson Library in December 2008.

The opening and re-naming of buildings is always a time for celebration and there have been many notable events over the years. These include the renaming of the Harold Martin Botanic Gardens in recognition of the former Registrar and Secretary; the opening of the Richard Attenborough Centre for Disability and the Arts by Diana, Princess of Wales; the naming of the Sir Michael Atiyah Building in recognition of his role as Chancellor; the Frank and Katherine May Lecture Theatre, which gave the University an opportunity to thank them for their tireless work for the University; and the opening of John Foster Hall on the Oadby Campus, named after the former Chairman of Council which provided students with a new residential facility that has been regarded by many as stunning.

The opening of John Foster Hall also gave the University the opportunity to reinforce its links with the local community; which has been part of a long-standing tradition in Leicester. Many of the University's staff provide important services for members of the local and regional communities. For example, members of the Medical School are not only to be found in the classroom, lecture theatre and laboratory but also on hospital wards, as well as conducting outpatient clinics and on duty in Accident and Emergency at the

Leicester Royal Infirmary. In a different way, the Richard Attenborough Centre, the University Library and annual Sculpture in the Garden Show also offer many opportunities for the wider public to come on to the campus to attend concerts, exhibitions and theatrical performances given by visiting artists as well as staff and students.

People are at the heart of University life and their achievements are regularly reported to Senate and Council. For example: Professor Peter Sneath was awarded a Fellowship of the Royal Society in 1995 following Hans Kornberg (1965), Winifred Tutin (1979) and Ken Pounds (1981). Dr Angela Lennox was awarded 'Doctor of the Year' in 1996; and Professor Stan Cowley was recognised by the Royal Astronomical Society, the European Geophysical Union and the University of Helsinki for his distinguished work in Physics. However, the most well-known member of staff is Professor Sir Alec Jeffreys who has won numerous awards and prizes for his work in Genetics, in particular for the discovery of DNA Fingerprinting. The University also recognises the importance of supporting its staff. For example, the Teaching Fellowship Award Scheme has helped to promote the importance of teaching for the career development of individuals. All Leicester's National Teaching Fellows initially received a University of Leicester teaching award.

Alongside the awards to staff are those made to students at degree ceremonies. By the summer of 2008 almost 100,000 people possessed a degree from the University of Leicester. While most of these are awarded to students, Honorary Degrees have also been awarded by the University since its inception. Many Honorary Graduates have local connections as well as distinguished careers in the public arena including: Malcolm Bradbury; Evelyn Glennie; Engelbert Humperdinck; John Rutter and C.P. Snow. Other recipients are perhaps less well-known outside the local community or in their own field but nevertheless have made considerable contributions that the University recognised. For example: Wendy Hickling who was the first person to be awarded a University of Leicester degree and who subsequently went on to serve for many years as a local Magistrate, as Chairman of a local NHS trust and as a member of the University's Council; Mario Illien who produces high performance racing cars; and Freda Hussein who is a former headteacher of an inner-city comprehensive school in Leicester but is also known as a former High Sheriff and for her numerous contributions to the local community, including the University. Distinguished Honorary Fellowships have been established in order to allow the University to make a further award to those already holding an Honorary Degree in recognition of their continuing outstanding service to the University. These have been awarded to a range of people including Sir David Attenborough, Lord Richard Attenborough, Sir Michael Atiyah, Dr Frank May, Sir Patrick Moore and Dr Helen Scott.

The University's Annual Report also provides examples of the rich catalogue of activities, events and occasions that give rise to celebration. Over the years, Annual Reports have made reference to innovative research, links with industrial companies, and the establishment of spin-out companies based on work conducted in the University. They have highlighted the publication of major books and articles that have changed the way in which people research and teach in a range of disciplines. Whilst there is much to celebrate in an individual year, there are also celebrations that occur on an annual basis. Among these are Freshers' Week, the annual RAG week when students raise money for charity, sporting achievements including the annual Varsity matches, regular functions for alumni including the annual Homecoming, and events for staff who have achieved 25, 30, 35 and even 40 years' service for the University. The pictures that follow illustrate just a fraction of the many celebrations in the University across fifty years.

Openings/Launches

1. Philip Larkin (distinguished poet, former Assistant Librarian at the University College of Leicester and the Librarian of Hull University) opens the University Library in September 1975.

2. The official opening of John Frears' House by its benefactor (Pro-Chancellor and Chairman of Council) on 28 June 1979.

3. The programme for the 'topping out' ceremony on 25 March 1977 for the University's Clinical Sciences Building at the Leicester Royal Infirmary (subsequently named after the former Dean, Robert Kilpatrick).

CLINICAL SCIENCES BUILDING,

The Royal Commission for Medical Education proposed that Leicester should have a Medical School and the decision to proceed was made by Parliament in 1970.

The Clinical Sciences Building, in which medical students will complete their training within the hospital environment following their period of pre-clinical training, is the second large building providing accommodation for the University Medical School. It is planned that eventually there will be an annual intake of 144 students and this building has been designed for 96 of this intake.

PROGRAMME.

1.45 p.m. Buffet lunch in the new building.

2.30 p.m. Mr. M.A. Baatz, M.A. the Registrar of Leicester University will perform the topping out ceremony and will then thank the builders. He will invite the assembled gathering to drink the traditional toast.

UNIVERSITY OF LEICESTER SCHOOL OF MEDICINE
CLINICAL SCIENCES BUILDING
LEICESTER ROYAL INFIRMARY

TOPPING OUT

FRIDAY 25th MARCH 1977

ARCHITECTS	PICK EVERARD KEAY & GIMSON, LEICESTER
QUANTITY SURVEYORS	MONK & DUNSTONE MAHON & SCEARS, LEICESTER
STRUCTURAL CONSULTANTS	ALAN MARSHALL & PARTNERS, BIRMINGHAM
CONSULTING ENGINEERS	JOHN MILES & PARTNERS (LONDON) LTD.
MAIN CONTRACTOR	R.G. CARTER (KINGS LYNN) LTD.
SUBCONTRACTORS :	
MECHANICAL	YOUNG AUSTEN & YOUNG LTD. LEICESTER
ELECTRICAL	N.G. BAILEY LTD. BRADFORD.

TOPPING OUT.

The exact origin of the topping out ceremony is unknown, but it has a place in the folk-lore of Ancient Scandinavia and Germany and probably came to Britain with the invading tribes from these regions.

In the early days a human sacrifice was made to placate the spirit of the timbers. The Anglo Saxons replaced the human sacrifice by tying a green bough to the roof. Ale was added to the ceremony in the Middle Ages.

Today the nature of the celebration varies greatly from country to country, but the broad outline remains the same. When the building has had its roof fixed, some decoration such as flags, garlands or a fir tree is added and a toast of beer is enjoyed by the builders.

Normally a representative of the buildings owner performs a token task associated with the fixing of the roof and then proposes a toast to the site workmen for their efforts in constructing a sound building. As the topping out takes place, a Union Jack is hoisted.

4. The 'topping out' ceremony for the Clinical Sciences Building at Leicester Royal Infirmary on 25 March 1977, performed by the Registrar, Michael Baatz. Those present include the Bursar, Freddie Sutton (front row, 4th from the left).

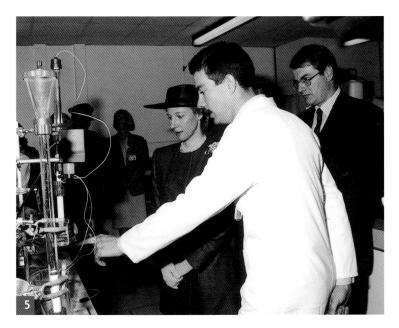

5. The Duchess of Gloucester being shown around the Breast Cancer Unit at Glenfield Hospital, Leicester, on 17 June 1991 by Ian Lauder (at that time Professor of Pathology) following the official opening.

6. Student musicians at the Richard Attenborough Centre for Disability and the Arts Building Fund Appeal in July 1991.

7. Sir Richard (later Lord) Attenborough with staff and students at the launch of the Richard Attenborough Centre Building Fund Appeal in July 1991.

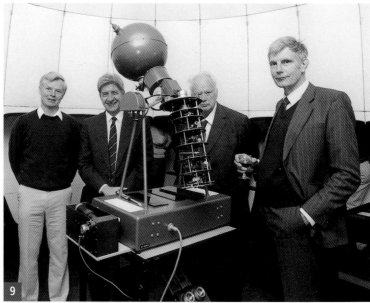

8. Opening of the University Chaplaincy on 21 October 1991 by the then Bishop of Leicester, Dr Tom Butler. Also present are the Roman Catholic Bishop of Nottingham, Dr James McGuinness, and a group of non-conformist clergy.

10. Naming of the Maurice Shock Medical Sciences Building on 10 November 1994, after the former Vice-Chancellor. Also present (l-r) are Lord Porter (Chancellor) and Dr Ken Edwards (Vice-Chancellor).

9. The opening of the University's Planetarium in the Bennett Underpass on 22 October 1991 by Patrick Moore. Also present (l-r) are Professor Ken Pounds, Dr Ken Edwards the then Vice-Chancellor and Dr Richard Jameson.

11. Naming of the Harold Martin Botanic Gardens in 1995, after the former Secretary and Registrar, who is speaking at the microphone.

12. Diana, Princess of Wales, being greeted by Richard Attenborough on her arrival to formally open the Richard Attenborough Centre for Disability and the Arts on 27 May 1997.

13. Diana, Princess of Wales, talks with an art student at the Richard Attenborough Centre.

14. The Rt Hon Estelle Morris (then Secretary of State for Education) talks with a group including Professor Marilyn Palmer (School of Archaeology and Ancient History) and Dr Paul Poplawski (Institute of Lifelong Learning) during her visit to Vaughan College to inaugurate the Institute of Lifelong Learning in January 2002.

15. Dr Frank and Katherine May at the official opening of the Frank and Katherine May Lecture Theatre, in the Henry Wellcome Building on 26 May 2005. This recognised their strong support for the University and its Medical School since the 1980s. Also pictured are (l-r) Professor Nilesh Samani (Head of the Department of Cardiovascular Science), Varsha Samani and Professor Sir Bob Burgess (Vice-Chancellor).

16. David and Laura Wilson with Professor Sir Bob Burgess looking at plans for the re-development of the University Library complex preceding the official announcement of David Wilson as the project's main sponsor in October 2006.

17. HM The Queen, accompanied by HRH The Duke of Edinburgh, returned to the University after fifty years to open the David Wilson Library on 4 December 2008. She is shown with Richard Everard, Vice-Lord Lieutenant, and Jennifer, Lady Gretton, the Lord Lieutenant of Leicestershire.

Open Days

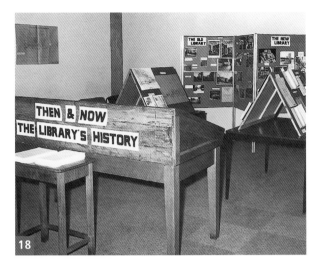

18. A display prepared for the University's Public Open Day in 1978 illustrating the history and development of the University Library.

19. A display showing contemporary developments in computer technology prepared for the University's Public Open Day in 1978.

20. A group of children taking part in an event at Jewry Wall about the Romans during the Open Day in March 1997.

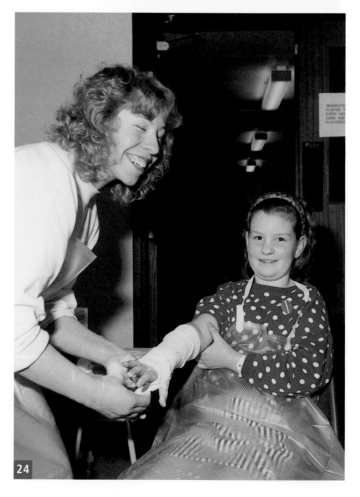

21. Members of the public participating in scientific activities at the March 1990 Open Day in the University's laboratories.

22. Prospective students attending the pre-Sixteen Higher Education Day in July 1991 being given a demonstration by Dr Jeff Sampson of the Department of Biochemistry.

23. A group of visitors to the 1997 Open Day discussing an exhibit by the School of Archaeology and Ancient History on what can be learnt from human bones.

24. A member of the University's staff demonstrating plastering techniques at the University's Open Day in March 1990.

25. Folk dancers on the steps of Beaumont Hall at the University's Botanic Garden Open Day in 1993.

26. Local girls, Victoria and Felicity Allen, with their cacti, from the Cacti and Succulent Society, at the University's Botanic Garden Open Day in 1993 in Oadby.

27. The sun was shining for the University of Leicester's largest public Open Day in over 10 years. A highlight of the University's 50th anniversary celebrations in April 2008, the Day attracted over 6,000 people, with staff, students, alumni and members of the public on campus to enjoy a wide range of activities such as the Viking Society who regularly meet on the Fielding Johnson lawn.

Sport

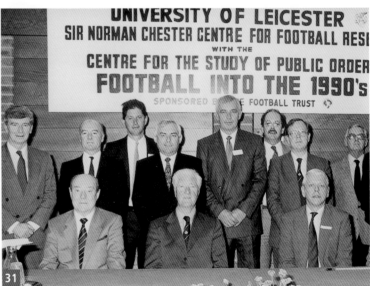

28. The Inter-University Women's Athletic Sports Medal, won by Leicester in 1963.

30. David Gower, Leicester and England Cricketer, trying out table tennis after opening the New Sports Hall in October 1987

29. The University of Leicester Cricket Team against former students' XI at a cricket match in June 1982 to celebrate the University's 25th Anniversary.

31. The Football into the 1990s Conference organised by the Sir Norman Chester Centre for Football Research and the Centre for the Study of Public Order.

32. Helen Young was selected for the Great Britain Triathlon Team to compete at the World Champoinships in the USA in August 1993.

33. William Sharman won British Universities' Silver at 60m at the Indoor Championships, February 2004, and British Universities' Gold at 110m hurdles at the Outdoor Championships, April 2006.

34-35. Women's Rugby Teams won varsity matches against De Montfort University at the Tigers Rugby Ground, Welford Road in 2005 and 2006.

36-37. Women's and Men's Soccer Teams won their varsity matches against De Montfort University at the Walkers Stadium in 2005.

Students

38. HRH Prince Philip talking to students at the opening of the Percy Gee Building on 9 May 1958.

40. Rose Nichols, the oldest language graduate of University College (with bouquet), visits the Modern Languages Department on the occasion of the AGM of Convocation in September 1993. Those present include Professor Mike Freeman (Head of the Department of Modern Languages).

39. Two new Leicester Graduates in the summer of 1992: Gary Lineker (Honorary MA, Leicester and England footballer) and Louise Wright (BA), with her guide dog Harmony. Louise obtained a First Class Honours Degree in Politics and Economic History and was the joint winner of the Maurice Hookham Prize for best Politics finalist.

41. Student guides ready to escort visitors around the University's Open Day for members of the public in 1993.

42. Overseas students at the Lord Mayor's Reception held in the City of Leicester in the autumn of 1993.

43. John Coleman preparing to receive his BA in English at the summer degree ceremony in 1996 assisted by his daughter, Dr Julie Coleman, who was appointed to the Department of English in 1995.

44. Richard and David Attenborough with members of the Students' Union Executive (Martin Cullen, Julia Coats and Simon Green) at the summer 2006 degree ceremony at which they received Distinguished Honorary Fellowships, the highest honour the University awards, for their extensive contribution to the University.

Visits

45. Presentation of 500 books on American culture donated to the University by the US Embassy Library. Those shown include (l-r) WW Hoffman (the US Consul), Marjorie Haford (Librarian of the US Embassy in London), Jack Simmons (Professor of History) and Sir Charles Wilson (Vice-Chancellor).

46. HM The Queen and HRH Prince Philip being shown the designs for the new campus on the occasion of the opening of the Percy Gee Building.

47. Students awaiting the arrival of the Royal car at the opening of the Percy Gee Building on 9 May 1958.

48. The Queen meets students at the opening of the Percy Gee Building.

49. The University Mace Bearer leads the Royal procession on the occasion of the Official Opening of the Percy Gee Building on 9 May 1958. Also present are Lord Adrian (Chancellor of the University) with HM The Queen, and Percy Gee (Pro-Chancellor) with HRH The Duke of Edinburgh.

50. Archbishop Robert Runcie looking at DNA Fingerprinting in the Department of Genetics during his visit to the University on 25 October 1986. Also present are Ila Patel (Technician) and Dr Nicola Royle (Postdoctoral Fellow).

52. HRH The Duke of Edinburgh touring the Space Research Centre on 26 February 1999. Also pictured is Sir Tim Brooks (the then Lord Lieutenant of Leicestershire, in uniform) and Professor David Llewllyn-Jones (Department of Physics and Astronomy).

51. Russian visitors in the High Bay Clean Room in the Department of Physics during their visit to discuss collaboration on a joint space mission.

53. The Duke of Buccleuch, Charles Nosworthy, the Duchess of Buccleuch, Claire Harding and Professor Andrew Millington (Department of Geography) during a visit to the University Library in the spring of 2000.

54. HRH the Earl of Wessex, Prince Edward, and HRH The Countess of Wessex, meeting a group of students and performers during their visit to the Richard Attenborough Centre on 3 September 2003.

55. The Band of the Gurkhas 'Beating the Retreat', organised by Councillor Derrick Horsfall, Mayor of Oadby and Wigston Borough Council, at Beaumont Hall, Oadby, in June 2005.

Awards

56. Sir Fraser Noble (Vice-Chancellor), James S Reynolds Jnr (Chairman of the Reynolds Metal Co, Virginia, USA) and James Gowan (architect) during a visit to the University's Engineering Building which received the Reynolds Memorial Award in May 1965 from the American Institute of Architects.

58. Richard and David Attenborough with members of their families following the Degree Ceremony on 1 October 1970.

57. Sir Fraser Noble (Vice-Chancellor) accepting the Reynolds Memorial Award for the University's Engineering Building in London in May 1965.

59. Richard and David Attenborough on the award of their Honorary Degrees on 1 October 1970 with their brother, John.

60. The presentation of the Royal Institute of British Architects' East Midlands Region Award for the new University Library on 16 December 1975. (l-r) Douglas Smith (President, Leicestershire and Rutland Society of Architects), Sir Fraser Noble (Vice-Chancellor), Raymond Kenning (Chairman, East Midlands Region RIBA).

61. The Procession of Chancellors of the Universities at the presentation of the Queen's Anniversary Awards at Buckingham Palace in February 1995. Those pictured at the head of the procession include Lord Porter (the University's Chancellor) with the Princess Royal (Chancellor of the University of London).

62. The presentation of the Queen's Anniversary Award for "World Class Teaching, Research and Consultancy Programme in Astronomy, Space and Planetary Science Fields". The Queen is shown with Dr Ken Edwards (Vice-Chancellor) and Professor Tudor Jones, (Head of the Department of Physics).

63. Sir Alec Jeffreys (Professor of Genetics) being awarded the Freedom of the City of Leicester in 1993. Also present are Dr Ken Edwards, Vice-Chancellor (left) and Henry Dunphy, Lord Mayor (centre).

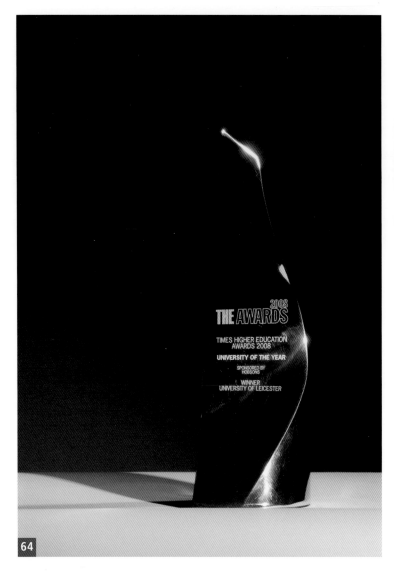

64

65

66

64. The University of the Year Award presented by the *Times Higher Education* magazine in November 2008.

65. The Centre for Labour Market Studies receives Investors in People status in 1998.

66. An informal discussion between members of the Genetics Department. Left to right Dr Annette Cashmore (Head of Department of Genetics), Professor Sir Alec Jeffreys (Royal Society Wolfson Research Professor in Genetics), Terry Lyymn (Departmental Services Manager) and Parvez Lokhandwala (Student on the MSc in Molecular Genetics) and HM The Queen at the time of the presentation of the Queen's Anniversary Award to Genetics for Research and Impact on Science and Society in February 2003.

Conclusion

When Leicester became a University in 1958, less than five per cent of the UK's population went to university. Fifty years on, almost fifty per cent now embark upon a university education. This increase in the student body has presented challenges for all universities, including Leicester, and has necessitated many changes to the shape of the campus, the content and style of the curriculum and the range of research. The essential values of University College and the University of Leicester have been enhanced by the scale of the compact academic campus on University Road. When staff and students talk about Leicester, at whatever point in time, one of the key phrases regularly used is "it is a really friendly place". This has been an enduring quality of the University that has transcended time and space and is at the heart of Leicester's achievements, as being happy at work and study makes staff and students want to do new things and encourages them to push the boundaries.

So what kinds of developments have occurred over Leicester's first fifty years? When Her Majesty the Queen visited the University in 1958, she opened the Percy Gee Building in a formal ceremony in the Queen's Hall, which was a major venue on the campus. Fifty years on, she returned to open the David Wilson Library which now forms the hub of the main University campus. Between these visits there have been many changes, not least to the physical site with three high-rise blocks constructed: the Attenborough Tower, the Engineering Building and the Charles Wilson Building. The Science complex was added in the 1970s to house Chemistry, Physics and Geology among many

other departments. Medicine and Biological Sciences developed across University Road with the addition of laboratories and classrooms from the late 1970s onwards, culminating in the state-of-the-art Henry Wellcome Building that was opened in 2005. All these buildings were essential to house many major educational advances through research and teaching. The University has also responded to major national initiatives through student growth, the introduction of new subjects on the higher education curriculum, the development of foundation degrees, engagement with employers, widening access and becoming involved in school-based education. The University of Leicester has therefore continued to strive for excellence in the competitive world of higher education and is now recognised as a leading UK university. We might, therefore, ask what are Leicester's achievements?

Numerous successes have been accomplished by a wide range of staff and students across the years and the University estate has also been widely recognised for high quality provision. Some of the key milestones include:

- Leicester is world renowned for the discovery of DNA Fingerprinting in the Department of Genetics by Professor Sir Alec Jeffreys who has won numerous awards including the Albert Einstein World Award of Science, European Inventor of the Year 2007, many Honorary Degrees and a Distinguished Honorary Fellowship from Leicester.

- The University has been successful in the Queen's

Anniversary Prize competition for Higher and Further Education where Physics won the award in 1994 (the first year of the competition's existence) for "its work on the development of major x-ray astronomy satellite instrumentation and on the research of chemical and physical processes, global warming and pollution". Genetics also won this highly coveted award in 2002 for "continuing innovative research coupled with high-quality training of scientists and the promotion of the public understanding of science".

- Leicester has been the only university shortlisted on three occasions for the *Times Higher Education* University of the Year award which it won in 2008 when the judges commented "few entrants embody the spirit of these awards more than the University of Leicester. Its triumph in this category at the third time of entering sends out a powerful message to the rest of the sector on the nature of constantly striving for excellence. Leicester's turnaround in the last decade has been extraordinary, and it is encouraging to note that the university has risen through the league tables without feeling the need to compromise on its widening participation initiatives."

- Many departments have achieved the Investors in People Award including the Centre for Labour Market Studies, the Scarman Centre (subsequently the Department of Criminology), Residential and Commercial Services, the Students' Union and the Department of Engineering.

- In the field of Marketing there have been several awards over recent years including the Heist Fundraising Strategy Award, the Meetings Industry Marketing Award Best Brochure, and the Heist Gold Award for Education Marketing. The Residential and Commercial Services have also obtained their own marketing award, the Meetings Industry Marketing Awards (MIMA) Best PR Campaign for the TOGs (Terry Wogan's Old Geezers/Gals) annual convention and calendar launch in 2007.

- Leicester's buildings have also attracted many awards. The Engineering Building (designed by Stirling and Gowan) is the best known building on campus amongst architects and is frequently visited by groups of Stirling enthusiasts and architectural students. The different libraries the University has created have attracted awards including a Royal Institute of British Architects (RIBA) Design Award for the first main University Library in the 1970s and a RIBA East Midlands Award for the David Wilson Library in 2008 together with the ProCon Leicestershire Building of the Year Award, alongside other accolades and prizes.

- The University has contributed to the development of the City. The Medical School has a strong presence in the City's three hospitals where staff and trainee doctors contribute to the delivery of leading-edge medical services. The Physics Department has contributed to a City initiative by being a founding partner of the National Space Centre which has become a major tourist attraction and educational facility.

The list of achievements is endless and we have focused on only some aspects of the University's success. To this could be added the wide range of community initiatives including the provision of adult education classes currently provided through the Institute of Lifelong Learning and the Richard Attenborough Centre. These are complemented by a wide range of academic departments who contribute to their discipline and, where appropriate, to the development of policy and practice.

So, where had the University reached in 2008? In its 50th Anniversary year, Leicester was consistently placed in the top 20 UK universities by league tables in national newspapers, through the National Student Survey on teaching and learning and for research grant and contract income. Members of the University have become increasingly ambitious and recognise that they cannot be complacent as such achievement has to be maintained through the same level of hard work that was put in initially. In essence, the University cannot rest on its laurels. Among the areas which the University is currently developing are:

- A £1 billion Development Plan for the campus from 2008 - 2028. This includes the construction of new buildings as well as the re-development of existing areas. It begins with the Students' Union in 2009 and will need to take in the re-development of the Engineering Building and the Medical Sciences Building which are now reaching the end of their natural lives.

- Modernising the academic structure which has been in existence since 1951. At that time, Faculties were considered appropriate for University College and, in turn, the University. However, developments in the size and complexity of higher education demand speedier decision-making and the delegation of responsibility – a system that Leicester brought together through the creation of four academic Colleges (Arts, Humanities and Law; the Social Sciences; Science and Engineering; Medicine, Biological Sciences and Psychology), headed by a Pro-Vice-Chancellor with an area of corporate responsibility.

- Striving to improve the University's research record by increasing the grants that are awarded to academic staff from the UK, Europe and worldwide, and the numbers of postgraduate research students attracted to the University.

All of this is planned to realise Leicester's biggest ambition: to build on its leading position in teaching and research by developing teaching quality, enhancing the student experience and growing the research base. This will be a challenge in an increasingly competitive market in an economic downturn. However, the University believes this is important for ensuring that future generations of students are well educated and fully prepared to enter the world of work to contribute to the economic and social development of contemporary society.

Leicester's success in the future, as in the past, will also depend on those who work in the institution and who contribute drive, enthusiasm and vision in equal measure. It is to these people the University owes its achievements and relies on their successors to continue to develop it in the future.

Glossary

AGM	Annual General Meeting
AVS	Audio Visual Services
BA	Bachelor of Arts
BAe	British Aerospace
Blackboard	Virtual Learning Environment for Interactive Teaching
BSc	Bachelor of Science
Bulletin	University of Leicester Internal Newsletter
CELI	Centre for European Law and Integration
CETL	Centre for Excellence in Teaching and Learning
CONTACT	Student Volunteering Society
CPU	Central Photographic Unit
CULN	Colleges – University of Leicester Network
DClinPsy	Doctor of Clinical Psychology
DNA	Deoxyribonucleic Acid – Genetic Fingerprint
DSocSci	Doctor of Social Science
DVD	Digital Video Disc
EdD	Doctor of Education
Facebook	Social Networking Site
GENIE	Genetics Education Networking for Innovation and Excellence
GP	General Practitioner
HAH	Hospital at Home
HEFCE	Higher Education Funding Council for England
HeSCA	Health and Science Communications Association
HM	Her Majesty
HRH	Her/His Royal Highness
LUCA	Leicester University Charitable Appeal
LUCENT	University of Leicester Centre for Enterprise
LUSH FM	Students' Union Radio Station
LUST	Leicester University Student Television
MA	Master of Arts

MB PhD	Double Doctorate
MBChB	Bachelor of Medicine and Bachelor of Surgery
MBE	Member of the British Empire
MEP	Member of the European Parliament
MIMA	Meetings Industry Marketing Award
MP	Member of Parliament
MRI	Magnetic Resonance Imaging
MSc	Master of Science
Mooting	Simulated Court Proceedings
NASA	National Aeronautics and Space Administration
NUPE	National Union of Public Employees
PC	Personal Computer
PGCE	Postgraduate Certificate of Education
PhD	Doctor of Philosophy
PPARC	Particle Physics and Astronomy Research Council
RAC	Richard Attenborough Centre
RAG	Raising and Giving – Student Fundraising Activity
RIBA	Royal Institute of British Architects
Ripple	University of Leicester Student Newspaper
ROSAT	Roentgen Satellite
SPLINT	Spatial Literacy in Teaching
UCAS	Universities and Colleges Admissions Service
UHL	University Hospitals of Leicester NHS Trust
UK	United Kingdom
ULAS	University of Leicester Archaeological Services
USA	United States of America
VISTA	Visible and Infra-red Survey Telescope for Astronomy

References

Amis, K. *Lucky Jim*, Harmondsworth: Penguin Classics, New Ed edition, 2000

Beck, A. and Willis, A. *Crime and Security: Managing the Risk to Safe Shopping*, London: Palgrave Macmillan, 1995

Bradbury, M. *Eating People is Wrong*, Harmondsworth: Penguin Books Ltd, New Ed edition, 1962

Broadhurst, K. and Benyon, J, *Gun Law, The Continuing Debate about the Control of Firearms in Britain*, Scarman Centre Occasional Paper Series, Paper 16, Leicester: University of Leicester, 2000

Bullock, B. *Over the Wall: A Working Class Girl at University in the 1950s*, Studley: Brewin Books, 1998

Burch, B. *University of Leicester: A History, 1921-96*, Leicester: University of Leicester, 1996

Kadioglu, A. 'The Role of Streptococcus pneumoniae virulence factors in host respiratory colonisation and disease', *Nature Reviews Microbiology*, 2008 vol. 6, no.4, 288-301

Lam, M.P.H. Senior Women Academics in Hong Kong: a life history approach, unpublished EdD Thesis, Leicester: University of Leicester, 2006

McKean, J. *Leicester Engineering Department Building: Leicester University 1959-63, Stirling and Gowan (Architecture in Detail),* London: Phaidon Press Ltd, 1994

Royal Commission on *Medical Education* (The Todd Report), London: HMSO, 1968

Simmons, J. *New University*, Leicester: Leicester University Press, 1958

Townsend, S. *The Secret Diary of Adrian Mole Aged 13¾*, London: Methuen, 1983

White, P. *Developing Research Questions: A Guide for Social Scientists*, London: Palgrave Macmillan, 2008

Index

This Index is organised by topic and does not include the names of individuals, other than when they are used for buildings, lecture theatres and so on.